"En l'air!"
(In the Air)

BERT HALL

"En l'air!"
(In the Air)

The Experiences of an American Foreign
Legionnaire as a Pilot With the Lafayette
Escadrille on the Western Front and in the
East During the First World War

Bert Hall

LEONAUR

"En l'air!" (In the Air)
The Experiences of an American Foreign Legionnaire as a Pilot With the Lafayette
Escadrille on the Western Front and in the East During the First World War
by Bert Hall

First published under the title
"En l'air!" (In the Air) Three Years on and Above Three Fronts (1918)

Leonaur is an imprint of Oakpast Ltd

Copyright in this form © 2011 Oakpast Ltd

ISBN: 978-0-85706-725-8 (hardcover)
ISBN: 978-0-85706-726-5 (softcover)

http://www.leonaur.com

Publisher's Notes

Contents

DEDICATED TO MY COMRADES
WHO ARE STILL THERE, WHO HAVE MADE
THE SUPREME SACRIFICE FOR HUMANITY,
AND TO
MR. AND MRS.
LAWRENCE SLADE,
WHO HAVE BEEN FATHER AND MOTHER
TO US ALL——MAY THEY LIVE FOREVER!

Original Publisher's Note

This book is the amazing story, told in his own words, of an American who fought in the French Army from the second day after war was declared in 1914 until the present time. His service included also special duty on the Russian Front. The following citation, in the Order of the Day for the entire army, gives a glimpse of his remarkable exploits:

General Headquarters, June 18th.
Order No. 3083D.

The Medaille Militaire is conferred upon the following name: Bert Hall, sergeant of Escadrille N 124. Engaged volunteer for the duration of the war. After having served in the infantry, transferred into the aviation. Has become very rapidly *pilote* of the first class. Very intelligent, energetic and audacious. Has fulfilled on many occasions on his demand missions particularly dangerous and perilous in rear of German lines. The 22nd of May has attacked and after a very severe combat, destroyed, his adversary within a few hundred metres of our trenches. This nomination carries the *Croix de Guerre* and one palm leaf.

J. Joffre.

Wounded many times, twice severely. Lieutenant Hall now may wear when he chooses seven decorations, including the Cross of St. George, awarded by the Russian Government only in cases of exceptional bravery. This cross, pinned on the breast of Lieutenant Hall by Czar Nicholas, was the last decoration he gave before his downfall.

Lieutenant Hall was asked by the publishers for a biographical sketch, and sent this characteristic reply:

I was born at Bowling Green, November 7th, 1880. Have spent most of my life travelling and in foreign countries. Began sporting career by riding high jumping horses. Afterwards took up automobile racing, then flying. Was ten years in Texas, six years in Missouri, and about six years in France before the declaration of war in 1914.

The title, *En l'Air*, familiar to many American readers, is the command given aviators in the French Army to leave the ground on the duty to which they have been assigned.

CHAPTER 1

The Foreign Legion

It certainly is good to be back here in America again, but I expect to return to the Western Front soon. There is plenty to do, a job for every man who is able to walk. With me the great trouble and bother is that my right arm doesn't work the way it used to, but it is getting into fair shape again. The doctors have built up the part from the shoulder to the elbow so it really looks like an arm again. They've patched me up in several other places, too. They are wonders, these doctors, in the way they can make over a man, and in some cases I think better than he was originally.

But even at that your body isn't like your aeroplane. If the engine breaks, you just go get a new one and start out again. But with your arm, if there's anything left of it, you have to make use of what still works and let it go at that.

They may let me fly again, and I certainly hope they will. Naturally I prefer the air, for that is where I've done most of my work, but I've been in fighting of all kinds since I enlisted in the Foreign Legion of the French Army two days after war broke out in August, 1914 Since my return to this country many people have asked me why I joined the French Army, and my reply is that if a country is good enough to live in it is good enough to fight for.

I am just thirty-seven, but still feel able to whip any German on earth at any game he chooses. Over here, they tell me that I'm too old for the United States service. Over there, with the few of my comrades who are still living, it is different. So I must go back to good old France. May she live forever!

As luck would have it, I was in France at the beginning of hostilities. I don't know how it was with others, but all the Americans I knew in France couldn't be neutral.

We wanted to fight, and fight right away. Practically every American man I talked with in Paris wished to enlist and many of them did, as everybody knows. It was the second day after Germany's declaration of war that most of us, myself included, got into the game. Everything and everybody in Paris was wild, although the French Army was being mobilised in a very business-like way. So at first we didn't know where to apply, or what to do.

It was then that we made plans for organizing what we called the American Volunteer Corps. This movement was started by George Casmeze, who had lived in France for some years. René Philezot, Charles Sweeney and I were the committee chosen to get volunteers. We received permission from the Government to train in the grounds of the Palais Royal. Sweeney, being a West Pointer, was later one of our most valuable instructors. We got along very well and our enlistments went on fine. We had about one hundred and fifty, and they all seemed anxious to go to the front as soon as possible. Our training went on for two weeks or more, while the situation at the front was getting more desperate daily. This made us all the more eager to have a hand in it.

The day for our departure from Paris came on August 24th. I regret to say that some of our gallant heroes suddenly fell ill or had business elsewhere, but not more than is the case in most volunteer organizations like ours probably. I want to name here a few, only a few, of the real Americans who started out that day. I mention them for the reason that I knew them and also because we were to fight together, or in different branches of the service, in the months that followed. I am proud to have been among them, for they were the first Americans to join the French colours. Here are the names:

Charles Sweeney, James J. Bach, J. W. Ganson, F. Wilson, D.

W. King, William Thaw, J. J. Casey, J. Stewart Carstairs, E. Towle, Paul Rockwell, Kiffin Rockwell, F. W. Zinn, R. Soubirain, E. H. Towle, H. Lincoln Chatkoff, George Casmeze, Edgar J. Bouligny, Bob Scanlon, Dennis Dowd, George Del Peuch, Charles A. Beaumont, F. Morlae, A. Segar, F. Capdevielle, Charles Trinkard, F. Landreux, Bert Hall.

From Paris we were sent to Rouen. While waiting there we had our first taste of what was coming later. We were about seven hundred, garrisoned in an old machine shop. We slept on a brick floor, underneath the benches, and, as we had very little straw, the floor seemed pretty hard. We received our first uniforms which were known as fatigue uniforms. They were made of duck, pretty hard and scratchy, but answered the purpose. We also enjoyed our mess, as most of the boys were used to high living and, after the hard work that we were doing, a can of soup and a chunk of tough beef tasted pretty good. Here I also discovered that it does not take long to harden a tender stomach.

We had been at Rouen four days when we received orders to join our regiment at Toulouse. The trip was a novel one for most of the boys. We spent the fifty-five hours of the journey in ordinary box-cars, about thirty-five to fifty men in a car. These French box-cars are only twenty feet long, so you can imagine that we were a little crowded during those two days and three nights. There was no straw or hay, only the hard boards to sleep on, but all the boys seemed contented.

At Toulouse we detrained and awaited the arrival of our regiment from Morocco. This regiment is called the *Deuxieme Regiment Etranger*. We sure opened our eyes when they arrived, all nationalities and colours. We soon made friends, however, and got along nicely. Most of them were hard customers; they would steal anything from a cancelled postage stamp to a modern dreadnought.

This Foreign Legion dates back to 1812. It was formed in Morocco because most of the members would not be permitted to live anywhere else. They were murderers, robbers and crooks of all descriptions. So they were kept in Morocco where they could only work on each other. They were very good fighters, and, of course, kept in training, as they were continually fighting hostile bands of natives. These poor devils were nearly all killed off in France the first eighteen months of the war. This regiment was 4,000 strong, while an ordinary French regiment has about 2,000 men. I have learned since that it has been reorganized twelve times, which means that some forty thousand men have fought in it, practically every man killed or made prisoner.

We were put into the Foreign Legion to fill up the vacancies caused by some 1,800 Germans who were left in Morocco. The Foreign Legion was very popular with German and Austrian subjects, who preferred it to their own armies. Once in the *Estranger*, you were safe, they could not take you out. One was never asked any questions as to his origin. One could choose his own name. There were a few non-commissioned officers in the Legion with such names as Wagner and Friedman. They were good soldiers and have all been killed since in action.

Our financial affairs were the least of our troubles, I can assure you. We were paid every ten days, and they had us sign a receipt for the dime every time, just as if we were getting a million dollars out of a bank, instead of one cent a day, which was the pay we received at the beginning. If a soldier was issued a sack of tobacco, then he drew only seven cents on pay day instead of ten. We had been reading in the newspapers about the high cost of living and Billy Thaw said to me:

"I don't see why they complain, when they can go to the front and die on a cent a day."

About a year and a half ago the pay was raised, and the *simple soldat* or private in the French infantry gets five cents a day, a corporal gets 25 cents; a sergeant, 50 cents; a second lieutenant $32.00 per month; a first lieutenant about $45.00; and a captain $65.00 per month. In the aviation a corporal pilot gets fifty cents per day; a sergeant $1.50; second lieutenant about $140.00. Officers get double indemnity for flying, a non-commissioned man gets $1.00 and an officer $2.00 per day extra for doing the same work; a first lieutenant about $152.00, and a captain

WILLIAM THAW

about $190.00. You pay for your own keep and dress yourself, so as a matter of fortune you won't get rich, even in the Aviation Corps.

Our training at Toulouse was short, but very severe. It consisted principally of bayonet practice, shooting and field manoeuvring. There were a few long marches which was the easiest part, notwithstanding our seventy-pound load. We Americans trimmed up pretty well at the end. Some of the boys fell by the wayside owing to physical disabilities. On the day of departure for the front I think we only left two or three behind.

CHAPTER 2

At the Front

The day we entrained at Toulouse to go to the front everybody was happy. We had no idea where we were going, but
we were on our way! The trip in the box-cars lasted about sixty hours, when we found ourselves at Camp de Mailly. This
camp was a big one and close to the front, so that we Americans
were introduced for the first time to actual fighting conditions.
And they sure did give us some strenuous work-outs. We soon
learned why the French railroads number the hours from 1 to
24, and say 13 o'clock instead of 1 o'clock. And we worked right
through from 1 o'clock on Monday morning until 24 o'clock
on Saturday night.

Here, at Camp de Mailly, we received our first promotion. We
were made first-class soldiers because of our marksmanship. In
shooting practice we very seldom ever missed the bull's eye. That
is, Bach, Thaw, Sweeney and myself. This entitles you to wear a
red stripe on your sleeve, and is quite a distinction. Some of the
men had been in the Foreign Legion for fifteen years and were
not yet first-class soldiers.

At Camp de Mailly they got us out usually at 5 o'clock in the
morning, sometimes as early as 3. The first thing was a five-mile
hike to the manoeuvring grounds. There we would drill for a
couple of hours and then go on a sort of scouting expedition
over the hills, always through brush and forests. They split us up
and we would have half our force, the right, as opposing troops.
Then each force would try to get the advantage of the other and

A BEAUTIFUL SEA OF CLOUDS, AT ABOUT 12,000 FEET ELEVATION

attack. By this method we were taught how to protect ourselves. The country was uneven and the brush very thick. All this was great sport for our officers who were mounted, but for us, not so sporty. We were the goats. Doing this over thirty miles of rough terrain is not sport, and nothing to eat until you finished. We used to clear up a spot in the forest and put up our tents just to see how well they looked. Then we would take them down again and hike out for camp.

Most of our drilling was conducted by an adjutant, the highest non-commissioned officer in the French Army. He has more authority than a captain in the American Army, and you won't be leary of these boys because they are tough customers, and would put you in jail for six months if they choose, and no questions asked.

It was here that we learned about the custom in the Foreign Legion of having a *comrade de combat*. He is a sort of fighting side-partner. You and he are supposed to stay together always during action. The *comrade de combat* assigned to me was an Italian by the name of Conti. He told me that he had been out of jail only nine days during the last eight years. Before joining the Legion he had been a bicycle thief to begin with. He said that this did not pay him well enough, so he took up grave-robbing, and found that a much more profitable business. I made him believe that I was a much worse character than he was, so we got on fine. In fact, Conti and I became great friends before our training at Camp de Mailly was over.

Conti used to steal my knife on an average of twice a week, and would very probably try to sell it back to me the day following. On one occasion, in particular, I had received some chocolates from a young lady in Switzerland. As I did not want to open the package in the afternoon that I received it (all of my comrades would have wanted a piece and sweets are very rare), I hid my chocolates in my knapsack. Between the time I received it and night, it disappeared. Conti was sleeping peacefully, but I felt as though he had my chocolates. As we all carried big knives at that time I put my knife against his neck and awakened him and said:

"Conti, give me my chocolates."

He produced them. Stealing was second nature with most of these men.

One morning we were ordered to get ready to leave camp. At last we were ordered to start for the big show! All the Americans in the Legion were in pretty good shape by this time, but at that the first marches seemed hard to us. One hundred and sixty kilometres in four days, or about twenty-five miles per day. It doesn't sound long if you say it fast, but with a seventy-pound load to carry it is different. Some of the boys had sore feet and suffered very much, but they were game and hung on. They did better than some of the old timers. Bill Thaw suffered most. His feet were swollen up like Zeppelins, and they were not like Cinderella's feet at the beginning, either. But he stuck it out, game old Bill.

At last, after passing through a totally devastated country, with absolutely nothing left standing and thousands of graves everywhere, we commenced to realize the seriousness of the war. This country had been torn to pieces by the Huns as they retreated. People in America cannot realize the devastation in France until it is possible for them to see it. You will find cities of ten thousand up to thirty-five thousand population where it is impossible for you to discover a trace that a town has ever existed. There; will be great difficulties in France after the war, for people locating their property, as there are absolutely no landmarks; and all records have been destroyed in these cities, so that they have no means whatever of tracing or locating their property.

Several times at night we would be aroused by German raiders, small groups of seven to fifteen Germans who had been cut off and were caught inside the French lines. As this country is all wooded they kept in hiding during the day and came out on raiding parties at night to get something to eat. They caused a great deal of annoyance to us, as French troops were often ambushed by these bands, many of which were cavalry. We found one German soldier hiding in a chimney who had

BERT HALL RETURNING FROM PATROL

Taken by a comrade. Clouds very low, an idea of desolation on the battle front.

an arm shot off. He had plastered mud on the stump and it was healing very well. He was afraid to surrender as he thought he would be killed. I believe it was three months before they were all captured.

After detouring a great deal we finally arrived at the front line near the Aisne, about 3 o'clock one afternoon. The place was Verzenay, near Rheims. We remained three days at Verzenay, without much sport of any kind outside of catching a spy who was signalling to the Germans with a light. No need to tell what happened to him.

On the morning of the fourth day we were ordered out of Verzenay and that same night arrived at Cuery des Chaudes Arbres, near Craonne and Cromwell, where there had been quite a bit of fighting recently. Our company was chosen as advance guard and we started out to find the Germans, but they found us first. Here we got under fire for the first time. The Boches had sent an aeroplane over us and when it had signalled back the firing began. They did pretty well, too, as they were shooting at about four miles distance and we were behind some hills. Some of the shells came very close, but the boys didn't seem to mind them much. Shells are not so bad if kept at a certain distance, but very unpleasant if too close. Bill Thaw used to say when one came whizzing past:

"Wish I was home," and then we would all forget it until the next one came along.

During this, our first experience under German artillery fire, it was amusing to watch the actions of the men. We were in open country, mostly sugar beet fields, and I saw men get down on their hands and knees and put their heads under the beet leaves. As long as they could not see out they felt perfectly safe. While we were marching up there were about fifteen of us posted as an advanced guard. Among them was one of our short-legged friends whom I will not mention by name, and he was very much inconvenienced by the German shellfire. We were marching in single file, as in that manner you are not as easily detected as if marching in larger formation. Jimmie Bach and I walked up alongside of this friend of ours and when we did so, he began to walk faster. We would increase our gait, keep up with him, then he would slow up and then we would slow up. Finally, he said:

"Go ahead; don't you know the Germans can see us easier when there are two or three together?"

We said: "We don't care."

We were about four miles from the German lines at that time. With this same young fellow we had some very amusing experiences later on in the trenches. As soon as he got there he seemed to have lost a great deal of his fighting spirit. The first thing that happened to him was that he could not see in the trenches. Then he got rheumatism, but was finally placed as telephone operator, and afterwards he was sent to Morocco for reasons unknown. One day, after a very heavy bombardment when we had lost quite a few of the boys, he came up to us for sympathy. No one would sympathize with him. Finally, as a last resort, he looked up one of our German corporals, by the name of Wiedman. He was very busy working on one of our dugouts that had been damaged by shellfire and he said to this old German:

"This war is terrible, isn't it? So and so has just been killed."

The old corporal, without stopping his work, turned to him and said:

"Oh, that's nothing. It's probably your turn next."

And at that he almost fainted. There were very few of this type among us and it didn't take long to get rid of them.

It was nearly dark on the day that we finally arrived at our post, and then we had a march of over four miles to the trenches which had been assigned to us. The mud was up to our knees. During the march Jimmy Bach and I pulled one of our short-legged friends for two miles through the mud. Some pull. We finally got him there all right. We piled into the trenches about 10 o'clock that night, and the regiment we relieved seemed glad to get out.

The trenches were a new game for us. We couldn't see a thing, and we didn't know in what direction or how far the Germans were from us. As a matter of fact we were too tired to do much investigating just then. Almost the first thing we received orders not to talk or smoke. That was tough we thought. We didn't want to talk and we didn't mind being shot at, but not to smoke was too much. Naturally, being worn out, we all went to sleep. I was chosen as sentinel in our trench and I looked around for the Germans. I could not see any, so I decided I would sleep a little, too. We had left our guns up on the parapet. I draped myself on top of my pals and had about started to go to sleep when I thought it would be best to take the guns down for fear the Germans might come up and steal them. I did this and felt much easier in my mind. Once I was awakened by a shell that came screaming over our heads. Then the breakfast call, but no breakfast.

The trenches had been very hastily made so we started out the first day to improve them. Believe me, you can dig some when the shells are falling all around and your digging is very essential to your health. The German lines were about nine hundred yards away.

During our first morning in the trenches a few of us were called out to shoot at some Germans who were chopping wood. Back of their lines, probably twelve hundred yards from our trenches, they continued to chop, and did not seem to mind our fire at all. Finally we decided they were too far away to do any damage so we went back into our trenches without getting any results.

During the day we were very heavily shelled, and, of course, we lost a few men. We continued our work, however, until we had very good trenches and very comfortable ones, well covered and dry. We remained in these trenches for the first period of eight days, and lost only a few of our boys. Then fresh troops were moved in and we went out.

In the trenches, we spent our time reading, talking and sleeping when possible. Also killing *to-tos*. We could not play cards as cards were scarce and we had no money. Playing cards without money is not a man's game. We used to talk mostly about eating. That sure was our most popular subject. As soon as you mentioned something good to eat, someone would tell you to shut up, not to talk about such things as we would never eat again, and we did almost get out of the habit.

The *to-tos* were our most popular form of sport, at first. That's the French name for them, and some people call them seam-squirrels, or just plain vermin. I think the *to-tos* must be of German descent, as each one carries an Iron Cross on his back.

They get to be pretty good-sized if permitted to thrive. We had nothing to kill them with so in a few days we had some good big ones. We used to have names for them, such as Gyp the Blood, for they were always bent on murdering someone by degrees. I had one I called Lefty Louie because he limped; he had a bad left leg. I could feel his limp when he walked. We were also bothered by rats. When we first saw a rat we used to feed him, but soon we found that we had made a mistake. Almost overnight they were with us by the thousand. They would eat your shoes and run all over you at night.

Between the rats and the *to-tos* there was little sleep to be had. However, we were all very well satisfied with trench life. Things began to wake up about 1.30 in the morning with the kitchen detail. This was made up of a corporal and from seven to eleven men. They were detailed to go back to the kitchen, which was about four and a half miles in the rear, to carry up the food for the day, coffee, cold meat and bread. Each man got half a loaf of bread, a big slice of meat, and one pint of coffee. We had to carry this for four and a half miles in mud up to our knees, dark as it possibly could be, and if by any accident you slipped and fell, one hundred and fifty men didn't eat. We had to watch our steps or else get abused by our comrades. Being in pretty good health I was generally chosen to carry the bread. Seventy-five loaves weighing two pounds each, in a large sack, was some job twice a day. You never know what you can do until you try.

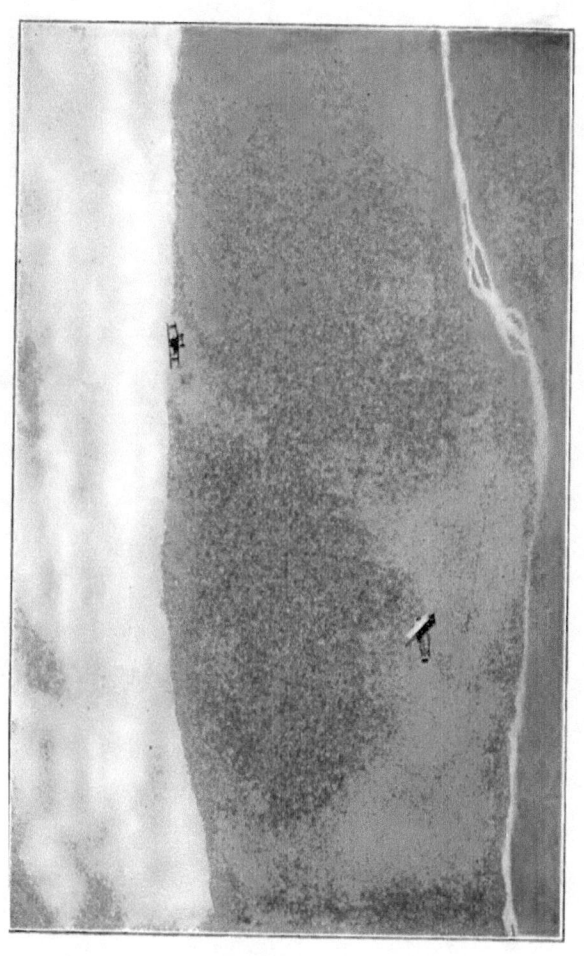

FRENCH OBSERVATION MACHINE AT LOWER LEFT, BEING CONVOYED BY A NIEUPORT

The white line in the foreground is a river.

CHAPTER 3

In the Trenches

Life in the trenches isn't all carrying bread by day or killing *to-tos* by night. We very soon learned that.

We had hardly got used to it when my squad was chosen for advance guard work. I could give a technical description of it, but it consists of standing in a hole half full of water for thirteen hours, one hundred and fifty yards in advance of the trenches in No Man's Land. You are to signal anything that happens during the night. Bill Thaw, Bach, Landreaux, Charles Ollinger, Stewart Carstairs, Corporal Morlae and myself were chosen for duty the same night. It passed, however, with nothing of any note. We could see the Germans putting up wire entanglements, but they were near their own lines. We were instructed not to shoot until ordered.

So, without a general order, which was given sometimes, we went out on scouting parties of only four or five men. If we had been permitted to shoot we would have been killed by some of our own men, as we were in front of our own trenches. The Germans, as long as they were near their own trenches, did us no harm. The artillery did all that kind of shooting. We were only there to repel an attack on our trenches, or to carry out one on the Boche trenches, and to signal any movement the Germans might make.

It was about 3 o'clock one morning, I should think, when our squad got out into No Man's Land. We very soon saw six shadowy objects moving near the German lines. They were obscured by some brush, and everyone was sure it was a German attack. They all wanted to shoot, but I insisted it was not wise. If we had fired we would have been fired upon by our own comrades and killed. I had some difficulty in making them desist from shooting but succeeded. As the objects came nearer we discovered that they were six cows! Morlae went out to see if they were accompanied by any Germans, as they sometimes used things like this for a blind. As Morlae approached, he was attacked by a gentleman cow in the party and beat a hasty retreat back. The cows were the only enemy we sighted all night.

Toward 5 o'clock we were to go back to our trenches and we started promptly. I happened to be the last, and as I was going across the open ground I was fired upon. When I stopped to see what the trouble was I felt a breeze on my face and realized it was another bullet going by, intended for me. It came from our lines to the left. They thought I was a German. I decided very quickly to lie flat on the ground, and commenced to fire back. I thought if they wanted to fight I would accommodate them as I was there for that purpose. An officer appeared on the scene and stopped our little war. I crawled to the trenches and was congratulated by my pals for having carried off the honours by firing the last shot.

We had another night or two of quiet, when a new sensation developed—a peculiar creeping sensation, sort of itchy. It was our old friends the *to-tos,* now too numerous to be funny. Millions of them, and absolutely no relief in any way; no change of clothing nor disinfectant of any kind. They are terrible, one cannot rest or sleep a moment. I discovered one remedy that would give relief for a few moments at a time. I had on three shirts and when the *to-tos* got well assembled on the inner one I would change it, putting it on the outside. This kept them hustling to make the trip down and up on the inside, which took them almost an hour. I would sleep during that time. Some of the boys went insane from the vermin; you cannot imagine how terrible they are.

We suffered, too, very much for the want of cigarettes, which

GERMAN FOKKER FLYING OVER FRENCH TERRITORY ON VERY CLEAR
DAY AT 12,000 FEET

You may see roads and fields of different colours. The machine was brought down (see next picture) in less than five minutes after this was taken. One of our machines photographed him, and we then brought him down. Machine fell in village seen in this picture.

is one of the most essential things to a soldier. I much preferred a cigarette to a meal during some of the days in the trenches, and both were scarce.

We were generally called out two or three times a night for an attack that never came off. I was always glad, for Stewart Carstairs, the only one who had cigarettes, would say:

"Bertie, let's have a smoke as we might be killed and this may be our last."

I said yes, and would crawl in and smoke. I was always glad when an attack was signalled as I was sure of a cigarette.

On the eighth day we left our trenches for the two-day rest period. They called it a 'Vest," and it was a fine one—march all night in the mud, arrive at 7 o'clock in the morning, sleep in the mud, then dig trenches until dark; do this for two days, get bombarded just the same as in the front-line trenches. On the night of the second day we were off again to some new trenches which had to be strengthened. We were continually shelled and bitten by *to-tos*. This new trench system was called Piccadilly Circus. It was some network, more complicated than the streets of Paris dare be. You would get lost very easily if you could not see the marks.

Afterwards we marked them all with names like streets. We built up these trenches also, which seemed to be a sort of pastime for us. They were about five feet deep, three feet wide at bottom and two feet wide at top, covered over with big timbers or anything we could find, and about two feet of dirt on top of that. There were port-holes for our guns. It requires three men per yard on the front to do this work, so you can imagine how many men it requires for the six hundred and seventy-five kilometres of front in France.

The Piccadilly Circus trench system was built under very trying conditions, and our troops suffered heavily from shellfire. Probably forty *per cent*, were killed. In the particular trench where Jimmie Bach and myself were, we had a sort of a rise just where we went out. So one day we decided to dig that out. Jimmie got his pick and started to dig. About the second stroke, he picked out part of a human head. So we decided we'd leave it there.

While we were in these trenches we lost a great many men. We used to go out and bury them at night. It was very easy as our cemetrey was in a big bank just back of the trenches. So we would just dig a notch in the bank and bury them standing up. It was much easier than digging an ordinary grave.

While we were here the first snow fell. Bill Thaw and I decided to catch a few rabbits, as we were hungry; so we proceeded to go out and find some wire to make snares. The only wire available was a small telephone wire used in the trenches. So we tore down the telephone line to make rabbit traps, and we heard the results of our demolishing the telephone line, but in language that cannot be expressed here.

We lost about as many men by shellfire when in repose as we did when in the trenches, as there was absolutely no protection for us. One gets used to those things, sort of a matter of fact. When one hears the shells coming there is not much danger; it's the ones you don't hear that get you. Then, too, you can get trained so as to be able to tell about where a shell is going to fall. By listening one can hear them coming quite a distance; they make a noise like a hot iron being thrust into water. Small shells make very little noise; it is only four-inch or larger that make much noise going through the air. The actual explosion is not as terrible as one would imagine. Some of the German *Krupps* had four distinct explosions. They were constructed in such a manner as to explode at very short intervals, which made them more effective than ordinary shells.

This life of ours in the Foreign Legion continued until winter came on. Early in November the very cold weather began with five inches of snow. This added a new hardship, for some of the boys got frozen feet and suffered very much. We did not have any medicines, only opium pills and iodine. No matter what your ailment was, you got one or the other. We were pretty short on food in these days, too. I do not know the reason for this, but during November I can tell you that we didn't overeat.

SAME GERMAN AS IN PRECEDING PICTURE BROUGHT DOWN BY THREE FRENCH
MACHINES, INCLUDING HALL'S

Pilot killed, observer slightly wounded

As the weeks went by, with constant fighting. No Man's Land between our lines and the German trenches became a terrible place to look upon. There were many dead, both French and German, some of whom had lain there four or five months. It is a black picture, that landscape full of shell-holes, which, in turn, were often full of what were once the poor devils who faced each other, who went over and never came back. But the Legion didn't fare any worse than the other regiments, and war is war.

From the 17th of October until the middle of December, I never washed my face and hands. I never had my shoes off and no change of clothing of any sort. But I used to shave regularly, as I never could stand whiskers. We had coffee brought up in the morning about 3 a.m. and as I never drank coffee I used to use mine to make lather and shave. Some days we had absolutely nothing to eat. There was no drinking water to be had, as there were numerous dead lying all over the country.

Until December 14th, 1914, I remained with the Legion. Then three of us were transferred into the aviation. Bill Thaw, James Bach and myself.

CHAPTER 4

Training in the Aviation Corps

We jumped right into our new work in the Aviation Corps. It was what we had wanted right along, so there were no heartbreaks on our side when we bade a fond farewell to the Foreign Legion that 14th day of December, 1914. A lot of my pals were no longer where I could say goodbye to them anyhow. Many of the boys were already buried God knows where. And we never did know what happened to others. I had long ago lost sight of Conti, my *comrade de combat.* I am sure, however, if he has been taken prisoner that he will steal all the *Kaiser's* decorations eventually.

Aviation, we soon discovered, is a whole lot more than flying. Our experience showed that time, and a heap of it, is required to develop the men and to make an efficient corps. To say nothing of millions. Aviation is really two organizations, and they are kept separate:

(1) The front fighting units.

(2) Schools of entrainment.

At the front, aviation is divided into five separate branches. First, machines that regulate artillery fire. Second, bombarding machines. Third, photographing. Fourth, reconnoitring. Fifth, the fighting machines.

The front fighting units are under the command of the General Headquarters Staff, like other branches of the army. The schools of entrainment are directed by the department of the

Minister of War. Naturally we went to school first, for our A B C's. And it was about the tightest little school we could hope to see. Our course of training began at once. I was put on a small monoplane which had a 20-horse-power motor. The wings of the plane had been clipped. About all I did at first was to roll around on the ground.

Very soon, however, I was able to make the old thing go in straight lines, and then I felt that I was a sure-enough flyer. It wasn't so easy at that, for it is very difficult even for an old hand with these short-winged machines. When a man shows some improvement at this kind of practice he is given a higher-powered machine. With this he can roll along at about sixty miles an hour.

When your man is capable of handling this new machine properly, he is sent along to a full-grown one, equipped with a 25-horse-power motor. In this he can get up a few feet. Then he does some straight line work until he is sent along to the next class, which trains in a machine that will get up about fifty feet. Now he begins to get the feel of the air. He is perfected in this work until he is easy doing it, and his confidence begins to come. For his next step, he is given a 6-cylinder, 45-horse-power machine. In this he branches out a bit, doing more straight lines, and learns to turn. He also does figure eights, and gets up to about three hundred feet.

Now you think you are sure some aviator, and they put you into a 50-horse-power plane. It's five hundred feet up for you then, and you practise doing spirals with the motor stopped. The last stage in the proceedings is an 80-horse-power machine where you train until you go for your military license.

The test for your license consists of one voyage in a straight line to a specified point and return, about 100 miles in all. Then, after that, you do a triangle of 200 miles, passing two specified points. Your next stunt is to stay one hour at above 7,000 feet elevation. This terminates your training for a military license. If the man who has done this successfully proves also to be an apt flyer he is picked for a fighting pilot. If not, he is sent out on a two-seater which is slower and easier to fly. If chosen for a fighter, he is trained on the rapid machines and when perfected is sent to the acrobatic school where they are taught all sorts of stunts, such as looping, *vrilleor*, tailwing slips, and all the modern stunts. This training is very essential, for it enables an aviator to protect himself in combat.

Now comes the fighting part of your training. Each man, as soon as he is fit, is sent on to the shooting school where they shoot at a moving target which is towed by an armoured motor boat at fifty miles per hour, also he is trained to shoot at small balloons and at moving pictures. Here he uses the same type machine which is used at the front. When he is perfected here he is sent to the superior *école de perfectionmet,* which is located in the army zone. From there he is sent on to the front. And I assure you these men are capable of defending themselves. This course requires about six months.

All the training for the first three months is done on monoplanes, no double controls being used as the men are learning alone. They get to go gradually and have much more confidence, and turn out to be much better pilots. Both systems have been tried, but this is by far the better. We did not get the advantage of this modern training as it did not exist in our days.

Bill Thaw and I were assigned to an *escadrille*, the regular formation of which consisted of six machines. They were rigged up so as to require twelve men, six pilots and six observers, one of each for each of the machines. Of course these machines weren't what we have today. As a matter of fact they took about one hour to climb to six thousand feet and were equipped with a machine gun. We also carried four thousand arrows, which were made fast on the landing chassis in cases that could be opened by a lever by the observer. We found that they were very efficient against troops or convoys on the roads.

I went immediately to St. Cyr, which was the headquarters of those days. Thaw followed a short time later, and after a few days Jimmy Bach joined us.

Upon my arrival at St. Cyr, I had no papers of any sort. I went

NIEUPORT ASSISTED BY A FARMAN ATTACKING A GERMAN MACHINE
He is the lower right-hand one——see crosses on machune.
Height 15,000 feer

directly to the commander's office and he asked me who I was. So I told him that I was an aviator. He looked through his papers and said he had no record of me.

'It is not my fault. I am here."

"All right," he said, and put my name on the books. I was sent out to the store-room, rigged out with a complete outfit, which none of the rest of the boys were fortunate enough to get. That is the result of being the fast talker. And at that time there was not as much organization in the French Flying Corps as there soon was.

We started training on Caudrons. These machines were used for regulating artillery fire and reconnoitring work. They were fair, not very speedy, but good climbers and good for doing stunts. Owing to a slight mishap I was transferred to Avor, one of the largest training camps in France. Thaw remained in St. Cyr. I flew a Farman biplane here. We progressed very slowly, owing to the shortage of machines. Many amusing incidents happened to us here; but very few were fatal. Such things as one machine landing on top of another and running into the hangars. Turning over was a daily occurrence and, strange to say, it was always the fault of the machine according to the young flyer.

One of the most amusing spectacles that I witnessed was a fellow on a roller. That is a machine that cannot fly. The motor stopped quite a way from the hangars. So he decided to start it himself. He climbed on the machine and started the motor. The machine started off so quickly that he did not have time to get in, and it made directly for the hangars. Then it changed directions just before arriving. It proceeded to run all over the field, causing everybody to run high until it finally ended up by running into a hangar and doing about ten thousand dollars damage to machines that were on the inside.

CHAPTER 5

The Lafayette Escadrille

Bill Thaw was the first of us to get off to the front, but I was there soon afterwards. Then it was that our real stunts began, and they came thick and fast as soon as the weather permitted.

Our organization, which was first known as the American Escadrille, was due to Norman Prince and no one else, in my opinion. We continued to call it the American Escadrille until the American Ambassador, Mr. Sharpe, asked us to change the name. He feared that our Government would object to the use of the name American. Then it was called the Lafayette Escadrille.[1] All Americans were sent to this *escadrille*, and we fought together, never being split up to fight in sections.

Thaw at first joined an *escadrille* near Lunevielle called the C 46. Bill spent about a year there, was made a sub-lieutenant and was mentioned in the Army Orders. In April, 1915, Norman Prince, Elliot Cowden and Curtiss came over. They had heard of Thaw, Bach and myself, who were in the Flying Corps, and came over to join. That was the beginning of the Lafayette Escadrille.

Very soon Bach, Prince, Cowden, Curtiss and myself were sent to Pau and put on Bleriot monoplanes. Prince was the first to finish, but he waited for Cowden and Curtiss, who were going on Voisin bombarding machines. The three went to Avor to train. Bach and I stayed at Pau, as we could not go on the Voisins. We continued to train on Bleriots, Morans and Caudrons until

---

1. *The Story of the Lafayette Escadrille* by Georges Thenault also published by Leonaur.

FIRST AMERICAN ESCADRILLE IN FRANCE

Left to right; Kiffen Rockwell, killed in combat; Captain Thenault; Thaw in his rear; Norman Prince, killed in accident; Lieutenant de Laage, killed in accident; Elliott Cowdin, dismissed on account of ill health; Bert Hall, on leave; James McConnell, killed in combat; Victor Chapman, killed in combat.

we were sent to the General Reserve near Paris. We continued our training on Caudrons there until we were detailed to train observers for artillery work in the region of Paris. This was very interesting. Dummy batteries were placed in different spots. We would take the men and fly over as the men located the batteries and marked them on their maps. We amused ourselves at this for a time.

We were then asked to go on the Nieuports, the first fighting machines brought out. Bach and I had the distinction of being two of the first twenty Nieuport flyers in France. The Nieuport was considered a very dangerous and difficult machine to fly, owing to its small wing spread. We found them excellent, and more stable than any machine we had yet used. Bach and I got along fine and were soon off with an *escadrille* of Nieuports, the N 38, in Champagne, near Chalons sur Marne.

In the meantime Prince and Cowden had gone to the V.B. 103 in the north of France. Curtiss was left behind, owing to physical defects. He had quite an amusing experience while training at Avor. He was a blond, rather tall and wore glasses, a slight German resemblance. (I mean no offense to the man.) While on a cross-country trip his machine took fire, as they frequently did. He was forced to land near a village and started throwing dirt on the fire. When the peasants arrived they took him for a German, and, as he could speak very little French, he was taken to the village jail and held until Prince came to his rescue two days later. Since then I have not heard of him. Prince did some long-distance bombardments, as did Cowden. He was credited with bringing down a Boche on one of these flights. They both received the *Croix de Guerre.*

Bach and I were in Champagne with Captain Bouche, one of the finest Frenchmen I ever have known. He did as much flying, if not more, than any man in the French Aviation. Lieutenant D. Harcourt, another fine man with whom I spent a year, later became the commandant of the *escadrille.* Lieutenant Harteaux was also one of my comrades. He has since brought down twenty-two Boches. Bertin, who is one of the oldest flyers in France,

Sergeant Mangot, who was taken prisoner with Bach, Adjutant Bayer, who was killed during the Battle of Verdun—all belonged to the *escadrille*.

Our work consisted in reconnoitring twice daily; sometimes we went as far as sixty miles back of the German lines, kept tab on all movements of troops, activity on the railroads, concentration of material and any new earthworks—everything that was going on. We also had two barrages a day to do. That consists of patrolling the lines to keep the German fliers from regulating their artillery fire. This work was very interesting, as we found a number of Germans and fixed them plenty. We also did photographing. The artillery fire is regulated by two-seated machines equipped with wireless capable of sending up to seven miles. The machine doing the regulating generally gets over the objective. About the third shot will hit the target, after they have received our wireless.

Aviators all keep an official book, in which we record every flight. This book is inspected monthly, stamped and signed by the commander. I think I can give the best idea of our work by quoting some entries from my book.

In Champagne, before preparation for attacks of September, 1915:

September 7th. Reconnoissance, Lieutenant Amrich, observer, depart 8 a.m., return 10 a.m. Route, Dontrien Pont Forgere Perthe Bethneyville and return. Very heavily shelled over Pont Forgere; nothing of importance signalled. Maximum height, 3,400 metres or 11,100 feet; duration one hour and fifty-one minutes.

September 8th. Same reconnoissance, nothing signalled; duration, one hour and fifty minutes.

September 9th. Reconnoissance. Lieutenant Bonnvay, observer; route Souain, Sommepy, Senide, Leffincourt, Frinse, Juneville Bethneyville, Aubrive. Duration, two hours and seven minutes. Height, 3,400 metres.

KIFFEN ROCKWELL, FRANCO–AMERICAN FLYING CORPS.
Killed in action September 23rd. Won *Médaille Militaire* and *Croix de Guerre* with two palms.

September 10th. Barrage, my mechanic as gunner. Met a German Aviatik over Mourmellon; attacked him and forced him down into his lines. Duration two hours; height 2,600 metres.

September 13th. Reconnoissance with Lieutenant Amrich as observer. Had a shell explode near us at 3,200 metres making several holes in our machine, nothing serious. Duration two hours and ten minutes. Height 3,200 metres. Weather good.

September 21st. Reconnoissance with Captain Bouche as observer.

Here we had an exciting adventure. We received a shell very close and had a piece of it weighing about two pounds stick in between the elevator and the fixed surface, making it impossible for me to move the commands. Thanks to the wonderful construction of my Nieuport we were able to come down safely and made a good landing. The duration of this flight was two hours, twelve minutes, and our height 3,600 metres. That same evening I broke the altitude record for a Nieuport with passenger and all equipment aboard, making 4,200 metres or 14,100 feet.

The anti-aircraft gun has been perfected so that at the present time they are capable of shooting up to about 33,000 feet. These guns are mounted on a table similar to a railroad turntable. The bottom of this turntable is a mirror. Above that is a sort of a telescopic affair by which they locate machines in the air. They do not have to keep a watch in the air for machines. As soon as a machine comes within shooting range of the gun, the machine will be shown in the mirror.

They have an instrument by which they get your exact altitude, also an instrument by which they find the number of feet you are travelling per second. Consequently, they time their shell accordingly, which is a sharpener used for any aircraft work, and sometimes at twenty thousand feet they can make you wish you were at home. Our small machines are very difficult to detect in the air, as we only have a little more than twenty-two feet from wing-tip to wing-tip. They pass out of sight at about ten thousand feet. That is, out of sight of the naked eye.

Other artillery has also been perfected in proportion. We have guns ranging from the French 75's, which is a three-inch gun, up to the 500-millimetre, which is a twenty-inch gun. These guns are located anywhere from 700 yards up to six and eight miles back of the trenches. They are capable of shooting from six to twenty-three miles. A long-range gun is not the big calibre gun. Our long-range guns are 280 millimetre, or eleven and one-fifth inches. These guns can do very active work at twenty-one and twenty-two miles. They are all directed by airplane and their accurateness is something beyond imagination. They can drop a shell in a thousand-yard circle at twenty-one miles. They concentrate for bombardments at present time from six to ten thousand of these guns on a front of five to six miles.

These bombardments are carried out methodically. The first work is for the small guns, for destruction of wire entanglements in front of the German trenches. They use a special shell for this work, which explodes about six inches from the ground. They also use something similar to chain shot, such as were used in Civil War days. They are two guns about twelve feet apart that fire solid shots. These shots are connected by about three good, big, healthy chains. They pass over No Man's Land two to three feet from the ground, sweeping out all the wire as they go along.

After the wire has been destroyed, in about two hours, they begin work on the German trenches, with the larger calibred guns. This will generally take about three hours; all this work is being observed by airplane. When they are sufficiently demolished, that fire is stopped and the curtain barrage begins. This fire starts about seventy-five yards back of the German trenches. The object is to keep the Germans from bringing up re-enforcements, and also to keep the ones that are left from getting away; when our soldiers take the German trenches they get all the Germans that are left.

Victor Chapman

Killed, June 21st, at Verdun, falling in German lines

CHAPTER 6

Flying and Fighting in Champagne

My real work was now to begin, as the great offensive of 1915 in Champagne was on. I got my chance, the thing I had been waiting for since the days I was rolling around the ground in a clipped-wing machine.

The weather was cloudy the second day of the offensive. Everything was in motion and we all knew what was coming. A pilot was asked for, someone who could do a reconnoissance at low altitude. I volunteered with Lieutenant Manigal. We went over the enemy lines at 3,000 feet, and were immediately attacked by machine guns from below. We received a few bullets in the machine, and also were attacked by several Boches. We had the satisfaction of knowing that we located German re-enforcements, and they were bombarded and forced to retreat. It made a most interesting sight. We could see the soldiers fighting in the open country, although the smoke from the artillery made this difficult at times. We were complimented by our General for this, as our information proved to be very valuable. The duration of our flight was one hour and thirty-nine minutes, and our height 1,000 metres.

This reconnoitring work is often very dangerous, and several of my pals were made prisoners while doing it. You go far back of the German lines and risk being made prisoner because of possible motor trouble, and also by being attacked by German airmen in groups. They try to cut off your retreat. The anti-aircraft guns are shooting at you continually and you are forced to go to certain localities to see if any changes are being made and to note all movements of troops and material. A part of your work is to photograph the objectives designated by headquarters.

Our general programme was something like this:

You are given a fixed portion of the front to cover, and receive your orders before leaving, if there are any special points where an attack is going on, you leave your field and climb until you reach the lines. Generally you are at 10,000 to 14,000 feet by this time. You continue to climb as you patrol your section of the lines; you keep a close watch for Germans above and below.

We generally climbed up to 18,000 feet or more, and continued to watch until we were attacked or saw a German below. You slow down your motor, try your gun, and down you go. If there is more than one enemy plane, pick out the nearest and go after him. You continue this for two and a half hours, when you return to the French field where you make out a report of all that has passed. Now you are free, you may go where you please, until your next turn. In bad weather we play games, read and gamble. Mostly gamble. Poker and bridge are the two leading pastimes of that kind.

One morning about 11 o'clock a German aeroplane came down in volplane and landed on one of our aviation fields. The pilot, a lieutenant speaking French perfectly, came up to the captain commanding the *escadrille*, and saluted. He asked for the loan of some gasoline, saying that they had lost all of their gas owing to a leak, but if the captain would be so kind as to loan some they would continue their journey. Of course they were made prisoners. This officer told me at once on seeing me that I was an American. He said that he had wintered in Palm Beach. He seemed to think it nice of me to help the French. On another occasion a fur glove was dropped in our lines. A few days later there came another glove with a note, saying, that the finder might as well have the pair.

I brought down a sassy German several days later. I had fol-

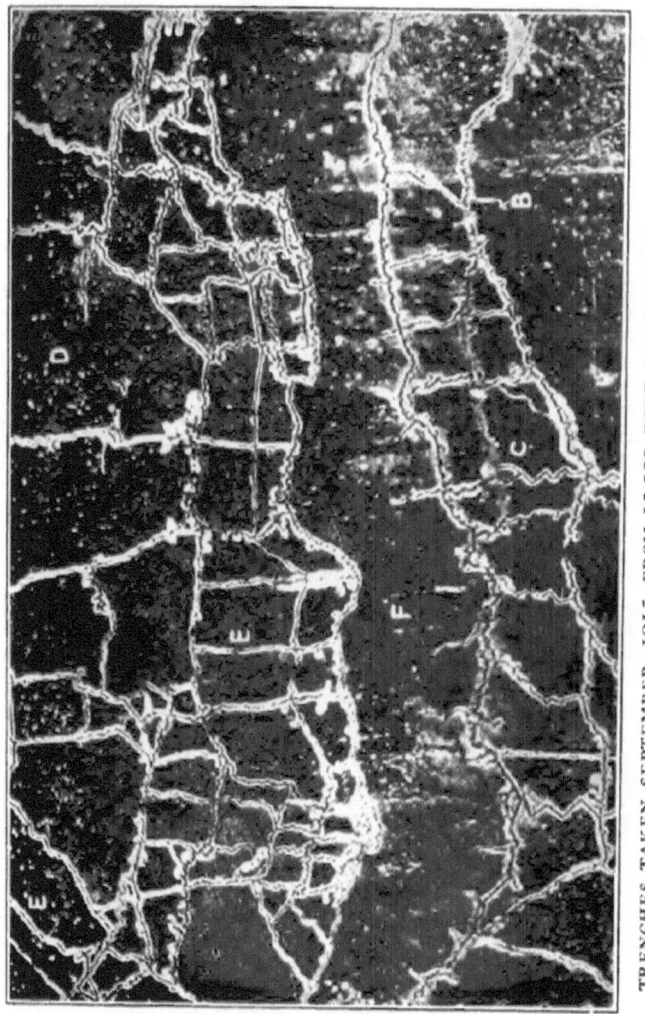

TRENCHES TAKEN SEPTEMBER, 1915, FROM 15,000 FEET ALTITUDE, IN CHAMPAGNE, EAST OF RHEIMS

B—Battery emplacement.
C—The French communication trenches.
D—All white spots are shell holes.
E—German trenches and communication trenches.
E (at top)—Road.
F—No-Man's Land.

lowed him for some time, but he did not see me. He was busy in finding a suitable landing place and his pilot was wounded. They landed and the observer helped get the pilot out. I landed very near him, about twenty yards away and got out. When I walked over to them they still did not notice me. Just as I arrived the captain-observer was lighting a match to set fire to the machine. I only had an instant to think, so I hit him under the jaw and out he went.

Very soon a number of French soldiers arrived and the two Germans were taken away. This officer was highly insulted because I struck him with my fist. I could not impress upon him that I did it out of politeness, as I could have shot him just as easy, but he could not see it that way. I got into the German machine, which was one of the latest type of Albatross, and flew back to my own field. They gave me two days' leave and I flew to Kieff in this same machine.

During the better part of September we found it almost impossible to go out, owing to rain and low clouds. I took a spy into the German lines with orders to leave him, and had a very narrow escape when I returned for him later. The Germans caught him and forced him to reveal our signals. They were waiting for me to return. When I was about fifty feet from the ground they started firing at me with machine guns, which they had hidden in some trees. My machine was badly punctured and I received a slight wound, but managed to escape and return safely.

Sometimes we would take carrier pigeons over to our men. For the work we had baskets and parachutes, and would go down to about one hundred feet. Then we would drop the baskets at fixed points.

A little later I went to Paris for a new machine, and almost missed ever coming back. I left Paris at 3 o'clock in the afternoon to return to my *escadrille*. It was cloudy, but the clouds were only about four hundred feet high, so I continued on my way. About forty miles out of Paris, I struck a terrible storm of wind, hail and rain, but decided to go on. It was impossible to see the ground and I did not have my compass. So I decided to have a look at the terrain. I started down and dropped to within fifty feet of the ground, but could see nothing that looked natural. Finally I saw a convoy on the road and went along slowly to see what it was. I discovered that it was German artillery. I turned around, but did not know in what direction they were going. That decided me to keep on at a very low altitude. I did so and soon saw a big gun in position. I took the direction in which it was pointed and found our trenches. I was pretty warmly greeted.

I landed again farther on and spent the night in a farmhouse, and I sure felt relieved to get back.

It was on December 18th, in a fight near Maschalt, that I got eighteen bullets, but the result of it was that I missed the Boche. So, on January 1st, 1916, they sent me to Avor for a rest. I put in my time there as an instructor, but did more flying than I had done at the front.

Victor Chapman was one of my pupils and I liked him very much. I spent two months at Avor. During the bad weather it was dull, for with no flying to do one gets bored.

RESULTS OF NIGHT FLYING
An English machine landed in a tree and
stuck there. No one injured.

CHAPTER 7

Fighting the Boche at Verdun

Work at the Avor training camp went on day after day, and for us instructors there was more work than we had at the front. However, it's very different training a bunch of lumbering recruits from the real game, and that's what any man wants. By Spring my rest was sufficient and I was getting good and tired of the alleged vacation they were giving me. About the middle of April I received my orders to start back to the front for active service again. So, on April 20th, 1916, I shook the dust, only it was mud, of the Avor camp off my feet.

When I rejoined the American boys they were at Luxeuil les Bains, and I found some new ones. Our first *escadrille*, or air squadron, was organized with the following men:

Prince, Chapman, Thaw, Cowden, Rockwell, McConnell, Captain Thenault, Lieutenant de Laage de Mienx, and myself.

Most of these boys have given their lives for the cause, God bless 'em, and I am proud that they were my pals. We were installed in a villa there at Luxeuil, and had to wait some time for our machines. We were attached to Captain Happe, one of the famous bombardiers. You get some idea of what he had done when I tell you that he had lost some thirty-five pilots that had gone to protect him. He was always lucky and escaped. He would talk to the boys, and tell us what to expect. Every one of us was willing to take a chance, which seemed to make him think a good deal of us. Captain Happe took only volunteers; he wouldn't have a man who went only because he had to go.

Our first interview with Captain Happe made a deep impression on some of the boys. We walked into his office as he was putting eight war crosses into little boxes. He cordially remarked:

"I am sending these to the families of the eight men I had killed in my last bombardment."

I guess some of the boys commenced to think that very soon their families would be receiving a small box also. But we were very lucky while with Captain Happe because we only lost two men. They were Norman Prince and Kiffin Rockwell, both great fighters.

The machines finally arrived, and then we started out to get the young fellows in shape. Our first patrol was on April 13th. The whole *escadrille* went out. Our orders were to patrol between the Swiss frontier and Cernay, about fifty miles east. We flew at different heights, from 12,000 to 15,000 feet. Jimmy McConnell went the highest, and he got lost. Jimmy was way over in Switzerland, and the following day we were notified to keep out by the Swiss Government. The next day we flew for the moving pictures. Around April 16th, Kiffin Rockwell brought down his first Boche near Thann. It was a singular coincidence that his enemy fell almost in the same spot where Rockwell himself lost his life eight months later. On April 20th, we received orders to leave at once for Verdun.

It was late in the afternoon when we arrived at Verdun, and we were immediately installed in our new quarters at Bar le Duc. The *escadrille* was put into action at once, and I can't say that our first sortie was anything excellent. We all went grouped, under Captain Thenault, and I flew next to him, about fifty yards to his right. He had told us not to attack until he gave the signal. Then we were to dive on the Germans. We had passed over three of their machines already, and we continued on into their lines. Just over Etain, some twelve miles inside the German lines, we saw six or more Boches.

The captain started to dive, and I also went down rapidly and picked out a German, thinking my comrades were all there.

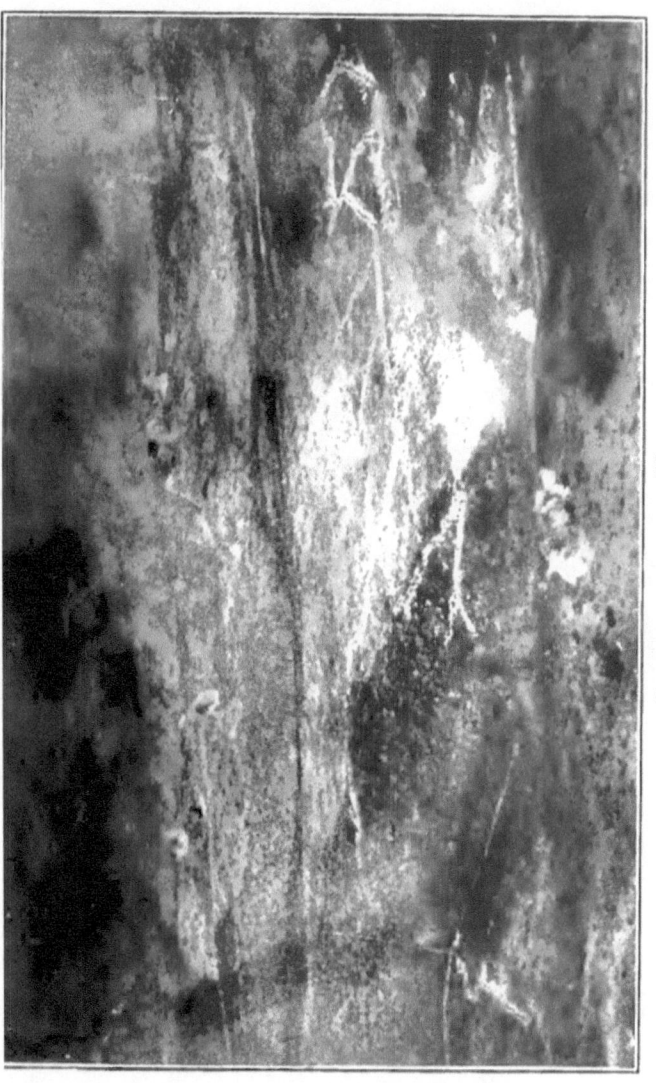

LOOKING NORTH AT VERDUN

Fort Douaurmont is near the white spot, which is shell holes. shells may be seen exploding along the line, and smoke up to six or seven thousand feet. White lines are trenches

But Captain Thenault had only come down a short distance and pulled up. He signalled to me that the others were not following. So there I was, left alone with Huns, not a very pleasant situation I assure you, I used up my ammunition quickly, as I only had 131 shells, and that didn't last long with a gun shooting 650 per minute. I did all the stunts that I could think of and finally went down as though I was hit. The Germans, thinking I was going to land, left me for a minute. Then I turned and off I went. With the slight start that I had I managed to escape. We commenced the fight at 12,000 feet and finished at 1,800 feet. I arrived O.K. after one of the closest shaves I ever had.

On the same afternoon I brought down a German at Malancourt, near Verdun. In this encounter we fought at 15,000 feet. I killed the Boche pilot and the whole outfit fell; nothing was left of machine or men. In this fighting around Verdun every trip meant a fight, and a good stiff one. There were a great many German planes, while the French had only a few good fighting machines.

I encountered Captain Boelke[1] daily. He had a Fokker fighter which was painted black with white crosses. The rest of the German machines were white with black crosses. Sometimes Boelke and I would do stunts for one another. I found that it was impossible to attack him, so I kept out of his range. A good pilot can always defend himself in a single combat affair. Boelke's pet prey were the old slow Reglage type of machine, those that could not protect themselves.

I had another interesting encounter with a Boche on May 18th. I followed him from over the forest of the Argonne as far as Nogent-sur-Seine, but I never could arrive at his height somehow. He was always higher than my machine would go. At last I was forced to land on account of running out of gasoline. The German went on, and dropped bombs on Epernay. He was at least 17,000 feet up. Our machines at that time would only

---

1. *Richtofen & Böelke in Their Own Words*, containing *The Red Battle Flyer* by Manfred Freiherr von Richthofen and *An Aviator's Field Book* by Oswald Böelcke also published by Leonaur.

climb to about 15,000 feet. That was also my first experience of having grenades thrown at me. When one is lower than the enemy machine they drop these grenades on one. The explosion is regulated by a time fuse; some of them came very close to me, but none were successful in hitting me.

On June 2nd, fourteen planes came over and bombarded Bar le Duc. I was alone at the field at the time, just starting out on patrol. I happened to look up; some Boche were just over my head. As soon as I could get my machine ready, I left the ground and was followed shortly afterwards by Victor Chapman and several other boys. We attacked the Boche and brought down one. Victor and I followed them and I assure you we made it very uncomfortable for them. They did a great deal of havoc, however. Seventy people were killed and two hundred wounded. Bombs fell within three feet of our hangars. On June 16th, the same thing occurred again, but we stopped them in time, and only a few people were wounded. On June 23rd, there were many combats, for the Germans kept up their furious activity in the air as well as on the ground.

It was here that we lost one of our best and bravest men, Victor Chapman. The combat occurred just to the north of Fort Douaumont. Victor was engaged with six or seven German machines and he hadn't a chance. He fought to the last inch and fell, dying, inside the German lines. Just where, I don't know. But some day I hope to find his grave and pay my respects to one of the bravest of the brave.

A little later, along in July according to the record in my official Aviation Corps book, I brought down my second Boche plane. This happened over Fort de Vaux. It wasn't really much of a fight, for I don't think that he saw me until it was too late. On July 27th, I had another one down to three hundred feet, but he escaped as I ran out of ammunition.

We suffered big losses in machines with the daily combats. At last the new ones came, and we were glad to discover that they were of a new model, each equipped with a 110-horse-power motor. They were rigged up for effective fighting, too, with a

GERMAN AEROPLANE BROUGHT DOWN NEAR VERDUN,
FALLING IN FIRST-LINE TRENCHES

See remains of machine on parapet of trench, wheels with crosses. Brought down by Lieutenant Dumas (since killed in combat) and Bert Hall.

machine gun shooting through the propeller. Best of all, they had a band of one thousand cartridges. They were faster and better climbers, and could make about 1,000 to 1,300 feet per minute, with a speed of 115 miles per hour. The guns on these machines were timed with the motor, so that the bullets did not hit the propeller. This very simple device, which never gives any trouble, was invented by a mechanic named Alcyon.

These machine guns were capable of shooting about 600 shots per minute. The propeller turns over at the rate of about 1,650 revolutions per minute. Consequently, with the two-bladed propeller that we used, the propeller blades were passing 3,300 times per minute in front of the muzzle of the gun. These bullets passed between the blades without ever hitting them. We used for this air-fighting what is known as a "cursing bullet." They are a great advantage to us, as we see every one, just where it goes. They look like small electric lights going through the air, leaving a trail of blue smoke behind them. To make an enemy machine fall, it is absolutely necessary to kill the flyer. If you put his motor out of commission he planes down and lands in his own lines. This is not counted as a machine brought down. As we are supposed to aim our guns with the entire machine, it is a great advantage to use these bullets, and we can generally put them where we want them.

On August 1st, I went to protect Norman Prince while he burned a captive balloon. This is done with a sort of sky rocket, three on each side of the machine. You dive head on the balloon, and when you are within fifty yards of it you press a button which ignites the rockets. They are rigged to burn for 600 feet, so if one of them struck the balloon it went up in smoke. Norman burned his and was mentioned in the Army Orders. On August 24th, I brought down another Boche near Etain, and on the 28th, I brought down another that burned near Fort Douaumont.

One day a German landed in our lines near Verdun. As everybody knows, the first thing to do is to destroy your machine to keep the enemy from getting it. Generally this is done by fire. But in this case the German did not fire it. As the machine was being examined, we found a sort of box underneath. When asked what it was, the German said that by pulling out a plug in the interior it would make a contact; there was a bomb in the box that exploded fifteen seconds later which would destroy the machine. We asked the German why he didn't pull the plug.

"This is a new invention, and I'm no fool," he replied.

During my service at Verdun I saw many of the big bombardments which were terrible. They are grand to view from the air. I have seen smoke up to 12,000 feet. The earth was one mass of holes. The whole country looked like a sponge. All the boys did well at Verdun. Thaw brought down two Germans. Lufbery (who had joined while we were there with Hill, Johnson and Remesy) got four or five; Lieutenant de Laage, one; Chapman, five; Kiffin Rockwell, five; James McConnell, one; Prince and Cowden one each.

OUR AVIATION FIELD AT VERDUN, TAKEN FROM 8,000 FEET

Hangars and some machines may be seen

Chapter 8

The Best Of Sport—An Air Sortie

"Start at 3 a.m. You are to go alone."

Every man in this war has, sooner or later, his great day. This was to be mine, although I did not know it at the time the order was given the night before. It was at Verdun and the date, according to my diary, was June 22nd.

Fighting had been going on around Verdun without interruption day and night, and many of the French aircraft were already victims of the enemy fire. At this time, as I now recall it, there were only six of our aviators in shape to take to the air for combat.

Our hangars were located in an open field eight or ten miles back of the great forts and front-line trenches. We had been cruising constantly for days, and cruising means good steady business, each man's daily patrol lasting about two and a half hours. It was our job to keep away the enemy aircraft, to protect the French photographers who went up on observation and topographical duty, and to note any changes in the German dispositions so as to direct and correct our own artillery fire. All of us were in trim for any kind of duty.

My orders for this particular day were not unlike the regular routine. It was cold and pitch dark when I crawled out of my blankets at 2 o'clock, which was really 1 o'clock, as the time is advanced in summer. My breakfast, like the others, consisted of rolls and coffee. As I do not drink coffee I concentrated on those rolls.

I made my way to our hangar and routed out Léon, my mechanic. In five minutes, with Léon's help, for it is something of a job, I got into my leather combination and boots, and climbed into my machine. On the side boots, and climbed into my machine. On the side of the car was painted in large letters:

BERT

My machine was a single-seated Nieuport biplane, driven by a 110-horse-power Le Rhome rotary motor of nine cylinders. In this type of engine the cylinders revolve around the crankshaft, which is stationary. My fighting equipment was a Vickers machine gun, and on this morning I carried 1,000 rounds of ammunition.

The sides and upper portions of the "Bert" were *camouflé*, to disguise it against the Verdun landscape. These decorations correspond exactly to the red clay of the soil and the green of the country—large, irregularly placed spots of both colours. Underneath, the "Bert" was painted sky-blue and bore the French insignia—blue, white and red circles.

An air sortie at dawn!

All was now ready. I settled myself in the seat and gave a once-over to everything as best I could—more by feel than by sight—as it was still dark. The machine gun was loaded and ready. On the ground, Léon was still puttering about, giving a last touch here and there.

"All set!" I called to him in English.

He understood, and started the motor. The blocks were still before the wheels of the machine, to make the final test of the motor. It purred smoothly. Then I gave the order. Léon kicked away the blocks. The "Bert" rolled along the ground for about fifty feet. Then I turned her into the wind and started up.

I left the earth in darkness. As the "Bert" shot upward I entered a world of soft light. Up here the dawn comes first. As it began to illuminate the Eastern sky, I pointed straight into it, thrilled and quickened by its inspiration. Soon I was able to make out the wooded rises in the ground and, as I went on,

BERT HALL AND HIS NIEUPORT, IN WHICH HE BROUGHT DOWN THREE GERMANS
NEAR VERDUN

His mechanic, Léon, since wounded by bomb, stands beside him.

the River Meuse became visible, seeming to flow out of the Boche lines. Sometimes, at this hour, the mist is heavy, making it necessary to wait and get your bearings. But this morning I was not held up; there was nothing to stop me from my work of concentrating on the field over Forts Douaumont and Vaux and the famous, bloody "304." The motor was buzzing along in fine shape and I was climbing at the rate of 1,300 feet a minute. The red old sun loomed up before me and, although it was still dark below, things began to get clearer but smaller.

A shell suddenly burst just underneath the "Bert," even before I was able to make out the enemy positions. The smoke was black, so I knew it was a German "Good morning" meant for me. Our own anti-aircraft shells make a white smoke.

I kept on ascending and very soon entered a cloud, one of those beautiful white banks as seen from the ground. It wasn't white, however—far from it. As I dived in everything became black; I couldn't see my hand before my face. The motor, which makes racket enough at all times, now sounded like a continuous, deafening bombardment. The cloud vapour, damp and thick, shut in every particle of sound. These "pretty white clouds" have no silver lining for the aviator!

Light ahead was welcome, and I emerged from the cloud with my ears tingling. The sensation is very much as if corks were popping inside your head in rapid succession. The wind was thirty miles an hour, or perhaps a little more. My altimeter registered 5,000 metres, or approximately 16,500 feet up. I had scarcely got into the open again and begun to search the landscape when there were more shells. They had seen me. I discovered that I was now directly over the German positions.

Naturally, my next move was to find out if there were any enemy aircraft in my neighbourhood. I looked all around, above, and particularly below, for that is the danger quarter in combat. I kept on and, when about a mile inside the German lines, I saw three machines far below me which had just taken to the air. I got up a little higher. They seemed to turn back, then one of them came on up. Soon all three were headed for me, the first having pulled away from his comrades.

I picked it out for attack and manoeuvred for position, eager to see what type of machine it was. As it came on I saw a fighting two-seater carrying a pilot and an observer. I managed to keep above, and it began firing long before they got near me. That is poor tactics and I did not mind. Rip went a hole in one of my wings, and then I did mind. But my turn was coming! I opened fire but could not tell if my bullets were going into the body of the machine. We both continued to fire and I was close enough to see the observer's face and square head as the machine rushed past. I looped-the-loop and as they went under me I put in a few shots for luck. Then the two-seater looped and I passed under it.

Suddenly there was *a rat-tat-tat* behind me. One look was enough. The other two machines had come up and opened fire on me. I pulled away to get into position again for the two-seater. As I did so I saw some red blotches on the wings of the "Bert." I knew that I had made a hit. It showed me, also, how close we had been to each other. The propeller revolving in front of the observer had spattered the blood on my wings. This proved that he was wounded in the face or neck. If it had been a body wound the blood would have flowed down to the boots inside the leather clothes, which are waterproof.

I again made for the two-seater, which had veered off, and, keeping up my fire, I passed within twenty feet of it. This time I saw the square head turned sideways, the body slipped down under the seat. He was dead. The machine began to descend, for, of course, the pilot could not shoot, and I did not see it again. My 1,000 rounds of ammunition was running low, but I decided that I was still good for another. Besides, I wanted to bring down a machine!

I didn't have long to wait, for the other two, both single-seaters like the "Bert," were on top of me before I knew it. One of them pulled off and I made directly for the other, letting my Vickers cut loose.

Twenty-five shots at twenty yards. That tells the whole story,

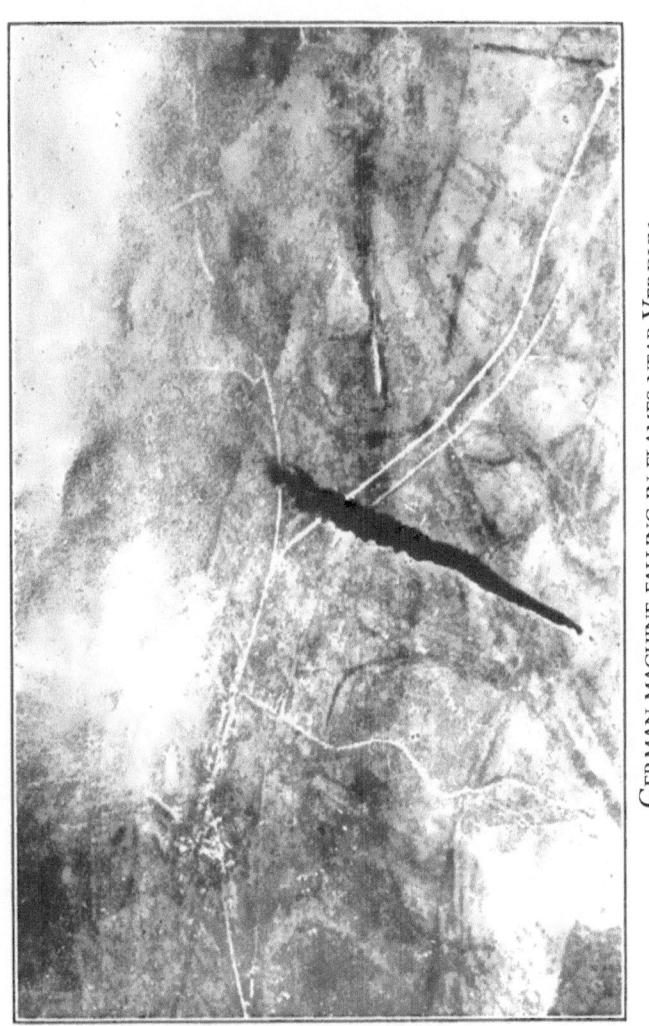

GERMAN MACHINE FALLING IN FLAMES NEAR VERDUN

Nieuport may be seen above the smoke. Aviators were burned. Taken by a French observartion machine.

and it looked like good night for me.

Suddenly, I saw flames bursting out of the cockpit of my antagonist—and I was saved. My aim, fortunately, had been true. Down went the Boche machine, a line of black smoke marking its path through the early morning light. I watched him until I saw him hit the ground. A puff of flame and smoke—that was all. I had brought down my machine! I was particularly happy because I had done it with almost the last of my cartridges.

Was I now alone in this particular chunk of atmosphere, or was the third Boche still a near neighbour of mine? I couldn't see him anywhere. I didn't know at this moment, but I think now, that the other single-seater which had pulled off was having motor trouble. Whatever it was didn't matter so much—*where* he was did trouble me, for in the air you must be ready for danger from six directions—from above and below in addition to north, south, east and west.

In order to find out what is below me I very seldom look over the rail of the car; in fact, it is almost impossible in a machine like the "Bert." So I just turned her on her side and got a good look below. No Boche. I had about made up my mind that the last of the three had gone home for breakfast when I suddenly discovered that he was nearly above me. I felt that he was about to try one of the pet Boche stunts—"getting under the tail" of my machine from above and behind. And he did. His gun, mounted in front, was aimed directly at me as he started on his behind-and-under dive. He had the advantage, for in order to hit him I had to turn and come at him head on, a *reversement* it is called. I tried this, and luckily the "Bert" responded so quickly that his bullets went wild.

As I had only a few cartridges left and I saw that my only chance was to manoeuvre—to do all the stunts I could think of, in fact—with the chance of catching him out of position when I was in. Also, I hoped that I might get on his nerves and if I could keep it up long enough I felt that he would turn and beat it for home.

It was like a duel, just fencing around for position. I looped and he looped. He set his machine gun and fired all the time. I kept away from head-on contact, so his fire was ineffective. I climbed and he climbed. Then I did some slips and *virages*, all the while manoeuvring for the moment when I could get in my last shots to advantage. But the moment never came.

I suppose the whole thing was only a matter of twenty seconds at most. Suddenly he dived and made off in the direction of the German aviation field to the east of Fort Douaumont. Enough is enough, when you are out of ammunition, and I had to let him go.

I looked at my watch; fifteen minutes more and my two and a half hours would be over. I slowed down the motor and prepared to descend, doing it slowly, for the air pressure constantly became harder on my head and ears. *Bang!* A German shell exploded not more than forty yards away. *Zim!* A piece of it ripped a hole, the second, in my wings. *Damn!* That's what I said, and didn't stop for any more. I was now passing over our own lines, and if ever the feeling of getting home grips you hard, believe me it's after you have been flying over German trenches.

The descent was gradual, for the reason I have said, but I was soon able to make out our landing field and hangar. One of my comrades, just starting up, passed waving his hand. I could tell that it was B——— by the number on the machine. I waved back, making a sign that I had brought down a Boche. One reason, and an absolutely necessary precaution, for the big number painted on the top and sides of the machines is to prevent slacking. We can always see the numbers and each of us is required to report movements that he witnesses. If any man declines combat, or refuses to attack an enemy machine he is sent to the trenches forthwith.

After passing B———, who never shirked anything in his life, God bless him! I came down to about 200 feet over our field. A short turn into the wind, nose down with the motor stopped, brought me skimming along at about a 90-mile clip to flatten out. Gradually losing speed, the wheels of the "Bert" finally touched the ground; then a turn, and up we rolled to the hangar without a scratch to show for our morning's work, save the two holes in the wings.

Léon welcomed me as I climbed out, cold and stiff, and pulled off my boots.

'Prepare yourself for a citation," he said, grinning.

"What?"

I was busy trying to warm up a bit and did not quite understand his broken English.

Then he went on in French, which I did understand.

"Balloon No. 49 has telephoned, *mon* lieutenant. They witnessed your fight. They tell us of the exact minute and location, of your Boche falling in flames. Prepare yourself for citation, and another palm leaf for your *Croix de Guerre*."

CHAPTER 9

Air Combats Along the Somme Fronts

By this time the Lafayette Escadrille was getting pretty well shot to pieces. The fierce flying and fighting in the Vosges district had now cost us, among many, two of our best, for Kiffin Rockwell and Norman Prince were both killed inside of a month of each other. The rest of us were still together and getting in some good licks on the Boche every day.

We received orders on October 14th to leave at once for the Somme. We arrived in good shape and I was mighty glad to find my old superior officer there. Captain Harcourt. He was now in charge of Escadrille No. 103, and it so came about that I was able to join him, which pleased me very much.

Work began at once in our sector on the Somme front. There was something doing every day. My first real stunt, a very short air combat, however, came on November 10th. I got the Boche at Raucourt, near Peronne, and brought him down clean inside our lines. He was piloting a German single-seater and I flew a Spad. The Spad is one of the later model fighters. It is a fine machine to fly and has more speed than the Nieuport. On the 14th I had a very close shave. This time I got a bullet in my cap, just nicking my head.

The bombardments here on the Somme were terrific. The artillery work had been concentrated to a high degree and was capable of firing 200,000 shells of all calibre per hour. This was

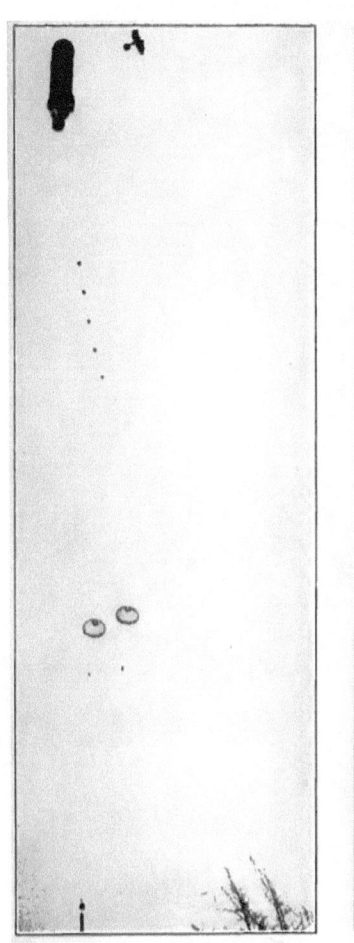

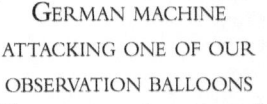

GERMAN MACHINE
ATTACKING ONE OF OUR
OBSERVATION BALLOONS

BALLOON FALLING IN FLAMES

The two observers here jumped and may be seen descending in their parachutes. No. 2 shows the results of this

equal to between nine and eleven thousand tons of steel and iron per hour, so you have an idea what it was like. It is a curious thing that one gets used to the noise, and I soon slept just the same as if I were at home. One night the Germans dropped bombs on our quarters about 2 o'clock in the morning. One of the mechanics was killed and many men wounded. The old shack was full of holes. A hangar containing seven machines was burned, and the Boche put about sixteen others out of commission; afterwards we got these planes in shape to use again.

On another night we got hit again good and plenty. The Boche did it with one well-placed bomb, too. This bomb was dropped on an ammunition depot where 100,000 shells were stored.

The shells exploded for ten hours afterwards, which was rather peculiar, only a few exploding at a time. They certainly made quite a little noise. Amiens was bombed at night, killing a large number of women and children.

These bombing raids at night were a feature of the fighting all that fall at the Somme. Of course we retaliated, going out after the Boche. It proved to be some of the most difficult work we had. It is almost impossible to see another machine at night unless you happen on it at very close range. Then it is very likely to be one of your own comrades. The risk to both pilot and machine is great—to the latter because landing is very difficult with a fast machine at night.

Otherwise our life at the Somme front was very agreeable. There were more than one hundred flyers of the fighting groups all on the same field. The formations here were called groups and consisted of four squadrons or *escadrilles*. Each one was made up of twelve flyers, four officers including the commanding officer and eight non-commissioned officers. Thus one group consisted of forty-eight machines. Each group was commanded by a major who fixed the hours and issued all orders. We had a regular routine of work, flying by patrol between fixed points, two hours and thirty minutes to each patrol. We went out once a day and were at alert for two hours and thirty minutes also. We were generally called out.

As our life here was typical of military aviation in general I will go into details a little. A man can figure on five hours a day in good weather. The most I have ever flown was eight hours in one day. A stunt like that is very tiresome and hard on a man because of changing altitudes so rapidly. A great many men have nervous breakdown or heart troubles and are sent to a separate hospital where they are treated by specialists and well rested before they are sent back. The life of an aviator at the front is very short. No one knows the exact figures, but I have heard it put at about seventeen hours of actual flying. The life of a machine is from seventy to one hundred hours, barring accidents. Strangely enough there are very few accidents at the front, and practically no loss of life by accident.

We were getting the newer and better types of machines by this time. They developed great stability in the air, the reason being that the centre of gravity is placed on the nose. You get the same results as from an old-fashioned dart, no matter what position the machine is in. You let her loose and she goes on her nose. Once there all that you have to do is to pull up and you are righted. I think this method of construction will be adopted by all manufacturers soon.

The men in my *escadrille* were billeted in small houses near the hangars and each man had a room all to himself. There was a large mess shack for the officers. We had our own cooks, who were professionals and generally good. We bought our own food, that is the officers. One man went back to some town daily and bought the supplies. The non-commissioned men were fed by the Government and they had plenty of food of excellent quality. There were two flying groups on this same field, so you see there was quite a crowd of us. We had a shower bath, electric lights, plenty of wood for heat, and a bar.

The benefits of the bar went to buy reading matter, and there was also a sort of casino where we played poker, bridge, and a few good old "prayer meetings" as the dice games were called. Money was the least of our troubles, as one did not expect to

GERMAN FOKKER BROUGHT DOWN IN OUR LINES UNDAMAGED
machine-gun may be seen with system for shooting through propeller

live long enough—so why worry about finance. We were all brothers and we discussed everything with each other, our battles and our love affairs. The aviators of France have the pick of the fair sex. Our *marraines*, or godmothers, sent us lots of nice things which were duly appreciated. We had moving-pictures once a week in a hangar, all the latest films.

We were given leave every three months for seven days. It sure was one continuous party from the day we arrived in Paris until the last minute of the third day. It made flying seem like loafing.

"Let's go back to the front and get some rest," we would say as we left Paris.

It's a fact that flying was so fascinating and so agreeable that we couldn't stay away from it long. I got homesick every time I had leave and I wanted to get back to my pals and the excitement. There is a fascination about it that ruins a man for anything else. I know that I will never be much good at work again.

Before I finally left for America I had, all told, three years of genuine sport. I don't know how much longer the war will last and my only idea is that I will have to go to work when it is over. I hate to think of it. Perhaps some kind philanthropist will put us on a pension. I hope so, as work would be an awful shock after so much pleasure and so many good times.

CHAPTER 10

My Methods of Attack

Usually it's all over in twenty seconds, one way or the other. My own experience has taught me that you have got to go to it quick if you pull out at all. One-third of a minute after contact with the enemy machine means victory or defeat, and in nine cases out of ten life or death for you. The reason is this: in that short time you have gained the offensive or else the Boche has. That particular air combat is as good as decided. The man who gets the offensive always wins.

I suppose every military aviator develops his own methods of handling his machine in manoeuvring and in attack. No two fights are ever alike and you are constantly meeting with new situations. Differences in altitude might seem to account for this in some measure, but this has not been true in my work. I have fought up as high as 20,000 feet and I can assure you that it is no different than a combat at 1,000 feet.

For fighting at high altitude we were well dressed, as the cold is very severe. During the winter months at 15,000 feet altitude it is about 50 below zero. When we are breezing along at the rate of 140 miles per hour it gets pretty fresh. We wear a seal-skin-lined one-piece combination, fur-lined boots, gloves and helmet. We have a preparation that we rub on our faces to keep the exposed parts from freezing. We also carry oxygen tubes, as the air is very rare above 16,000 feet. Your heart will stop working without oxygen. We have rubber tubes and when we get to feeling a little giddy, we stick this tube in our mouths and blow

REMAINS OF A GERMAN MACHINE BROUGHT DOWN IN THE VOSGES NEAR BELFORT

ourselves up. One charge of oxygen will last about fifteen minutes. At the end of that time, if you remain at the high altitude, you have to take another whiff out of the bottle.

One does not notice the altitude, only the lightness of the air makes one gasp for breath once in a while. The air is very calm above 10,000 feet, but in warm weather one gets shaken up pretty badly, up to 7,000 feet, by heat waves. In my own case I soon got used to flying, and I felt just as much at home in the air as on the ground. Sometimes we used to have to go at the rate of 1,000 metres to protect the artillery machines. Then one is in the trajectory of the big shells and they shake you up a bit. In one battle we lost several machines which were struck by our own shells.

I have heard Captain Georges Guynemer[1] describe his methods. He believed that the first twenty seconds did the trick. When in a tight corner his favourite play was looping the loop, for he had great faith in acrobatic tactics. He said he always tried to fly behind the Boche and below him if possible. I always felt better if I could get the altitude on an enemy plane. Guynemer was one of the best shots in the French aviation and he would bring his machine up short, after his opening attack, and open his deadly fire. In my opinion, to gain the altitude is to have the advantage. That is the reason, I believe, that so much of the work is being done so high at the present time. One can dive on an adversary and, by skilful manoeuvring, protect oneself to a certain extent from his machine-gun fire. There are certain positions from which he cannot shoot at once. If it is a case of a Boche single-seater one need not worry. You must watch his manoeuvring and not let him get behind you.

Sometimes we used a tracing bullet. You can see exactly where everyone goes and by this means repair your fire, which is a great advantage.

Unlike a single-seater, I have found that the big German double-seater is a mighty hard proposition. They are well armed and the gunner keeps a sharp lookout. One of your most tiring

1. *Guynemer Chevalier of the Air* by Henry Bordeaux also published by Leonaur.

duties is this business of lookout. You must keep constantly turning around to avoid being stepped upon.

Very seldom do you encounter a German who will fight you at equal odds. They are not clean fighters and cannot be classed as fighters man to man. They fight only in organizations. They are made to fight by discipline and not by overflowing courage. At the beginning there was some chivalry among them, but not anymore. Now we attack as soon as we see each other, and, of course, we are there for that purpose. The Germans cannot be compared to the French as fighters. Their machines are good but the men are deficient.

You soon find out that clouds are your friends, especially if the cloud is thick and full of holes. I did a good deal of this kind of fighting. You hang around over a hole and wait for the Boche to pass under, through the open space. Then you can get him by surprise from your ambush. It was in a battle of this kind that I fought at the heaviest odds I ever encountered, fourteen to one. It took place over Soully, the headquarters at Verdun, and Marshal Joffre saw the fight. I think it was one of the marshal's first opportunities to witness an air fight at close range, and he seemed to be much impressed by it. It was then that I was decorated with the *Médaille Militaire*, the highest French military decoration. This *médaille* cannot be worn by an officer, only by a non-commissioned man or general commanding an army. I was a sergeant at the time I was decorated with the *médaille*.

Many times, of course, there are attacks without results. Then we would each start back to his own lines, waving a hand for *au revoir*. If the pilot, or the machine, is hit badly it usually falls like a leaf, fluttering and zigzagging to earth. This is not always the case, for if the aviator stops his motor he falls slowly. If, however, the motor is running it generally falls nose first and at terrific speed. As a rule the wings buckle up and they go down like a stone. You can watch them until they strike the ground; a puff of smoke and a spot of debris, that is all. If the machine falls in our lines we generally land near it in order to get a souvenir.

Collisions in the air are more frequent than might be sup-

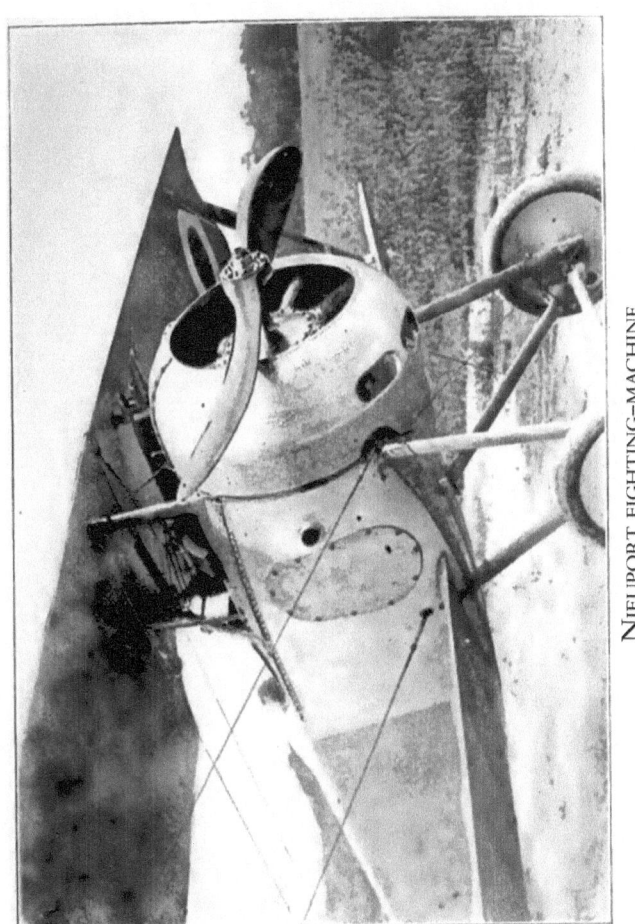

NIEUPORT FIGHTING-MACHINE

Machine-gun may be seen above motor

posed. It was at Verdun that I saw one of my friends, a French-man, misjudge in making an attack. He ran into the Boche and they both went down together for some distance. Then they came apart and fell to the earth.

That is not all. I have also set a German machine on fire, and unless you have seen such a sight you have no idea how rapidly an aeroplane will burn. It is horrible if you put yourself in the place of the pilot of that doomed machine, but you feel much better than if it were yourself. A long black train of smoke is all there is to picture the tragedy to you. The inflammable bullet is another weapon which is used with great effectiveness. It doesn't need to wound you to get in its deadly work. Once I saw a French captain whose machine had been set on fire by one of these inflammable bullets. The poor devil knew that he would burn before reaching the earth, so he dived into the German machine which was below him. They both went down together, burning. I have also seen a man fall out of a machine from an altitude of twelve thousand feet. He fell so rapidly that all one could see was a black line. There was nothing left of him, and his body was driven into the earth three feet.

Some people have asked me about this business of killing the other fellow. I can't speak for other aviators, but I never really wanted to kill another man—if he was a man. But you cannot call the German a man; he is only a savage. It is simply a case of getting him before he gets you. One is more of a professional than anything else, and it is different from the infantry. As I have said, there was at first quite a bit of chivalry in the aviation but that has ceased. We used to drop a line, telling the Germans of their comrades who had been brought down inside the French lines. If they were wounded, killed or prisoners, we would send word of it back to their comrades. When I bring down a Boche I am always relieved to see him go, as the more we kill the quicker it will be over.

Altogether I have brought down comparatively few machines as a result of the more than one hundred air combats in which I have been engaged. It is not as easy as it seems. One of the most distinct recollections you have of a fight is the noise of a machine gun in the air. Sometimes in a surprise attack, when you have a Boche slip up on you, the first thing you hear is the *tat-tat* of his machine gun. You can even hear the bullets go by above the din of your motor. That soon makes you get busy doing acrobatics to get away. We generally loop, like Captain Guynemer, if the enemy is near enough behind us. Then he goes under and we are behind him, which puts us in a position to give him his own medicine.

Nerve, after all, is the principal requisite of a successful military aviator. I have found that the best tactics is to go straight at the Boche. While you are doing this he gets a good chance at you, but if you have the nerve you get in more shots at him from a more favourable position than when you manoeuvre. You can only get in a few shots otherwise, as you are out of position when manoeuvring. I have tried all methods and find this the best. I have seen all the best flyers attack, Captain Guynemer, Navarre, Nungasser and the rest, for we were always together. Their methods of attack were different, but the straight dive always gave the best results.

CHAPTER 11

Submarined en Route to Russia

Early in December, 1916, the French Government received an urgent request from the military authorities in Russia and Roumania for some French aviators. They were needed on the east front, to show the Russians how we were playing the game, and also to put heart into their own flyers. It was now that a new phase of my work commenced. Orders came to me to go on this service, and I started at once for Petrograd, leaving Paris on December 19th.

My journey was full of adventure, including one new experience, an encounter with a submarine. From Paris I went directly to London, when I changed my French uniform for civilian's clothes. It is important to remember this. The ship I was to take sailed from Newcastle and our first port was Bergen on the Norwegian coast. On the way we were stopped by a German submarine. The sea was too rough, however, to permit the men from the submarine to board our ship. They held us a long time, asking us what our cargo was and our nationalities. If the weather had permitted them to come aboard I would probably have been taken a prisoner. I thank Providence for that rough sea. From Bergen we proceeded to Christiania, and thence to Stockholm.

Before reaching Stockholm I met up with a couple of Germans who were buying war supplies. Both were officers. They asked my business, so I said I was selling supplies to the Russian Government. So, being an American, they talked very freely with me. They were confident of victory and told me of their superiority in artillery and aviation. I said "yes," when I really wanted to strangle them. Thinking of some five or six Boches that I had brought down I decided that their superiority was not so great. They wanted to buy some things of me which I didn't have, of course. I asked how I could ship them. They replied that I could send the supplies to them at Stockholm where they had a house.

"We do quite a bit of buying in the United States," they told me. "Sweden is our friend."

I discovered this myself. I promised to call on them on my return from Russia. I would like to have done so—with a bomb.

From Stockholm I continued my journey to Haparanda, and across by sleigh to Tornes. It was forty below zero and the wind was blowing fifty miles an hour during most of the trip. At the Russian frontier I was examined by interpreters, and gone over most thoroughly, I can assure you. It took over two hours and I had a French diplomatic passport. They took no chances, for I was in civilian's clothes. More than once I thought I would never get through, and that is not all, for if an officer is found in civilian's clothes he can be shot.

The customs officials were very alert because many Germans came into Russia by this way.

Early the following morning I arrived at the Finland railroad station in Petrograd. The cold was terrible and I was glad to pay an extortionate price, ten *rubles*, to the taxi driver who took me to the Hotel de France. The ordinary charge is one *ruble*. At that time the *ruble* was worth 33 1/3 cents but before I left Russia its value had depreciated to about 17 cents. At the Hotel de France they gave me a very small room at ten *rubles* a day. There was no bath, of course, for baths are not very popular in Russia. In the morning I went down for breakfast, and when I saw the prices my appetite failed me. Eggs were one *ruble* each, bacon two *rubles*, coffee one *ruble*. The waiter only spoke Russian and, as I was not very apt at this tongue yet, we couldn't talk much.

"Do you speak German?" he asked.

HANGING OVER BIG CLOUD BANKS AWAITING A GERMAN TO PASS UNDER A HOLE AT ABOUT 14,000 FEET

"Yes," I replied.

Then he proceeded to talk in the most fluent German that I have ever heard. I am sure that he had been a *kellner* at the Winter Garden in Berlin and I know that his German was much better than his Russian. Like so many others he was a distinguished member of the *Kaiser's* secret diplomatic corps. They are all placed where they can do the most good for Germany. Only officers were placed in the Petrograd hotels where they could hear very important matters, for the Russians are not at all discreet.

The day I arrived in Petrograd, December 29th, was the day after the famous Rasputin had been murdered. There was crepe and other mourning emblems on many public buildings, especially the palaces. Rasputin and all his followers were pro-Germans and there is no doubt in my mind but that he was in daily communication with Germany. The influence of Rasputin in the administration of affairs was extraordinary. He controlled the railroads of Russia, and often the material assigned to the front for the armies never arrived. Whole train-loads of stuff were found in Siberia when it had been already to Petrograd and was consigned to the southwest and northern fronts. This was all the work of Rasputin.

Of all the wild tales about how Rasputin met his death, the one told to me by an officer of the Russian general staff is true. The monk was enticed to a village about thirty miles from Petrograd by three of his followers. He went disguised, as he knew his enemies were after him. He spent the day with these women. In the evening they suddenly disappeared and Rasputin found himself confronted by eleven men, all very noted personages in Russia, and among them one man who is very important in Russia today, (as at time of first publication). A revolver was placed on the table and Rasputin was told to kill himself. He did not do so, but picked up the gun and shot at one of his enemies. He missed the man and killed a dog that was in the room. Before Rasputin could fire again he was shot by three of the party. Afterwards they found three balls of different calibre in his body.

I spent only three days in Petrograd but that was long enough for them to politely separate me from nearly every cent I had. Prices were worse than the Klondyke in 1898. A glass of brandy cost $8.00 in our money. I am not a drinker so I didn't invest much in liquor. A pair of $5 shoes were $30 a pair. I went on my way thinking things would be better elsewhere, but I found just the contrary. The farther I went the higher the prices went. Everybody seemed rich but me. A clerk in an office that drew a salary of 100 *rubles* per month was living like a king. Once I asked a Russian officer how they did it. He smiled.

"Graft, my boy. You don't know Russia."

And I didn't. We Americans are three hundred years behind Russia. I really believe I was the only poor man there at the time.

A Nieuport protecting an artillery-directing machine above very light clouds Photo taken by an observer in a big machine, the struts of which are seen on the right.

Chapter 12

Trying to Help Russia
and Roumania

From one end of the Eastern front to the other was chaos, everything and everybody. The French officers who had been sent over were doing what they could to bring about order, and in spots things were cleaned up, put in shape and organized to some extent. It made me want to laugh and weep at the same time. My work took me from a point about one hundred miles south of Riga at the north to the very end of the Roumanian line on the Black Sea at the south. I had a chance to see what was going on everywhere, and I mixed with the officers and men of both armies, the Russian and Roumanian. I certainly was impressed with their ideas of war after my two years on the Western front. No system, no anything. They have eighty-eight national holidays in Russia and no soldier will fight on a holiday. The kind of fighting they do on the other days is a joke.

In the Russian aviation things couldn't have been worse. I found that the men would fly only when they felt like it. They almost never passed over behind the German lines. The average Russian aviator aims to fly six hours per month. His pay is two hundred *rubles* and after his six hours he takes a good long rest. When I started in to really do some flying they thought I was a patriot and a fool. In fact, they didn't make any bones about telling me so. They let the German machines do what they pleased; they flew all around our lines and were never molested by the

Russians.

Socially the Russian aviator is certainly a good fellow. They can all play a good game of poker and can put away a lot of drinks. I think they have the Germans beat in these branches. But as fighters they are *nil*. No patriotism, no enthusiasm and not too much courage. About all they did in the aviation corps was to drink champagne, play poker and "66," a German game. The men always say "tomorrow." They are never in a hurry and they don't worry. The Russian has no idea of what war means in the air. They are well equipped, having all the latest types of fighting machines. But the Russians are not air fighters. They were very frank, almost childlike, in expressing their feelings to me.

"Oh, we would be just as well off under German *kultur* as we are now."

I have often heard things like that. Russia means nothing to the average Russian, although I met a few, a very few, patriots among them.

From the north I went on down to the Caucasus front, and there I met the Grand Duke Nicholas. He is a remarkably able soldier and a patriot. He is fighting for Russia and is one of the few men who had any real influence with the soldiers. He is worshiped by his men.

One instance, a thing which happened to me, will show better than a description what the fighting was like here. It happened when I brought down my first Boche on the Eastern front. I saw him come over in our lines at about 1,500 feet altitude and I went after him. I suppose that he thought I was a Russian as he did not pay any attention to me. I proceeded to shoot him down. When I returned I was very much surprised to find that my comrades did not approve of what I had done. They said:

"We have been here a long time and the Germans have never bothered us. Now they will get mad and come and drop bombs on us and may kill some of us."

I thought that this was a little too steep, so I moved on to another squadron, but I found that they were all about the same.

Masson and Bert Hall

Our home on the Russian front
Aeroplane box used for house.

Soon after this I was proposed for the Cross of St. George, a decoration for officers only, which is very rare in Russia. I received it by the *Czar's* order only four days before he abdicated. It was the last one given out by him. I also received the *St. Vladimir,* which is the Russian *Legion d'Honneur,*

From the army of the Grand Duke Nicholas I went on south into Roumania, where I joined what was then the combined Russo-Roumanian army. I never would have believed such things as I saw there, and I doubt if the terrible story can ever be told. Out of the 650,000 men in the Roumanian army only about 90,000 were on the front. Everywhere the country and the people were in a most horrible condition. The greater part of this vast army had died of disease, although thousands of sick had been sent back into Russia to recuperate. Typhus did most of this slaughter. There was plenty of cholera, but that was fatal in only about ten *per cent,* of the cases. But here in Roumania under war conditions typhus was sure death both in the army and to the wretched civil population. The only chance you have with typhus is to be strong and well nourished. But there was not a man, woman or child in Roumania at this time who was in good condition, or anywhere near it.

The every-day scenes in Jassy were beyond belief. Jassy is normally a city of about 40,000 inhabitants. In it 450,000 poor wretches had sought refuge. There was no food for them and little or no shelter. They died in the streets by hundreds. Anything like burial or a quick disposition of the bodies was out of the question.

I couldn't get a meal and it seemed almost sacrilegious in the midst of all this horror to hunt for cigarettes. There were none, anyhow. But that was nothing. There was no soap, no sugar, coffee, tea nor clothing. To eat you only got corn meal cooked in a sort of mush and served cold. We had some beans but no other vegetables, meat sometimes twice a week. Not a bath house was open in the city. The cold was intense. There was no wood or coal for heat and the temperature was about twenty-five degrees below zero. Many of the doctors and nurses died of typhus.

The railroad station was converted into a hospital and in it were about three hundred beds. In each bed were three wounded men, and on the floor lay fully a thousand others.

I knew the French doctor here and he told me that they had no medicines and no food for the men. One day I went with him as he made his rounds in the station-hospital with his orderlies. They went along among the men, tapping them with a cane. If the man grunted they said:

"All right; he's alive."

If there was no response the orderlies would take out the body. Box-cars were used, the bodies being loaded into them and hauled out of the city. I saw three hundred at one time piled up awaiting burial. A great many died of hunger and from cold because there was no wood for heat. There was about three feet of snow on the ground. All winter communications with the outside world were nearly cut off. Only one railroad line ran to Russia and there was no organization on even this. It was not the same gauge as the Russian railroads and all stuff had to be transferred to Roumanian cars.

I often talked with French doctors who had been through the Serbian campaign and they told me that conditions in Roumania surpassed Serbia for misery and. suffering. There was absolutely no way of getting relief and news never left the country.

The Roumanian private is a good soldier, but the officers—zero. It happened that I arrived just in time to see General Souchec degraded and sent to prison for four years, Colonel Sturtza shot, and a good many others punished. Colonel Sturtza was going over to the Germans with his entire regiment when he was caught by a sentinel and made to confess. The French Mission straightened out a great many things like this. The Mission was headed by General Berthello who did some wonderful things for Roumania. Otherwise the Germans would have taken the rest of the country. Fourteen Roumanian officers of different ranks were executed. In the end a plan was adopted by which one French officer was attached to each Roumanian regiment. Their own officer had no value of any kind, only to paint his lips

Crowds in street during revolution, Petrograd

and powder his face. I will venture to say some of them go so far as to carry matches almost like men. They never go near the trenches. The Germans said that when they wanted a Roumanian officer prisoner they put up a barber's sign and he walked right into their trenches. There was no fighting on this front. You could go out and walk around the trenches and no one would molest you.

I was a witness here of what is probably the most terrible railroad accident ever known. It happened on the Barlade & Galata Railroad. A long train of about sixty coaches ran into another train, a freight, under suspicious circumstances. More than 1,000 persons were killed and 700 injured in the accident and the fire which followed. The engineer was an Austrian. He escaped and has never been caught so far as I know.

There was but one relieving thing about all this horror in Roumania. I met up with many of my old French friends here who had come over from Salonika or Russia before I arrived. I was presented to King Ferdinand, Queen Mary and Crown Prince Carol. They had eighty-six servants in the royal palace, and about fifty *per cent,* of these were Germans. They were well fed when the army was starving. I have seen their soldiers so weak that they could not walk for want of food. I gave them money, that was all I could do. The people would say:

"Look at our soldiers; no clothing, no food, no shoes, yet they never complain!"

There was a good reason; no one to listen to their complaints, so they did the best they could.

I also brought down a Boche here near Galatz on the river Danube, for which I received two decorations, that of *St. Stanislaus* and the *Vertu Militaire.*

CHAPTER 13

Bombing the Kaiser at Sofia

"Who would like to go to Sofia on a Bombing raid?"

The question came to us one morning, about the time that I had decided to get back to Petrograd. But I thought, why not get a glimpse of Bulgaria, just to add to my collection of Balkan impressions—about as unlike each other, and of as many colours, as a boy's sack of marbles. So I decided on the little jaunt to Sofia right then. Also, I was anxious to learn flying conditions in the Balkans, to see if they were anything like those to the north, or what I had experienced on the Western front.

A big percentage of the Balkan country is very rough and mountainous. Furthermore, it is not very agreeable to fly over because there are no landing fields. In case of motor trouble many people are under the impression that in rough countries there are air pockets and bad currents of air. There are to a certain extent, but with the modern aeroplane there is absolutely no danger.

The worst air disturbances in the Balkans, I found, are caused by heat waves on the very warm days. Up to 5,000 feet you are shaken up pretty badly, but in this rough country to find a place to land is difficult. There is not very much risk if you know how to do it. You may land on a tree and still do not hurt yourself. Maybe a few bones are broken, but not anything serious. But, if you don't know how, it may prove more serious, although our motors seldom fail us. There is no good in worrying. I have landed once off the aerodrome from motor troubles in three years.

In Roumania we had our field at Galatz, a town of about 40,000 population, on the Danube. The nearest point to the German lines was then about five miles. It was continually being bombarded. There is not much left of it now. Just opposite is Braila, a great grain-handling point. At Constanza and Braila, the Germans captured about twenty million bushels of wheat. We used to drop bombs on Braila daily, doing considerable damage, and I had already gone on some long reconnoitring trips. From here we used to follow the Bucharest line of the railroad to see what activity was going on.

It was beautiful country from the air. The Danube could be seen from the air for miles, but this Blue Danube stuff is all bunk. The river is as muddy as the Mississippi. There was a continuous patrol of armed tugs on the Danube, and quite a bit of shelling was done by these boats.

One morning (the date was Feb. 3rd), news came from Sofia that stirred up things in our camp and on the whole front near us. We learned that at Sofia there was being held a council of war attended by the Kaiser, Emperor of Austria, King of Bulgaria and the Sultan. We wanted to pay our respects to them with a few bombs, and we did!

Our route, of course, lay through Roumania, over Bukharest and so to Sofia. The morning was very cloudy. There were two of us for the trip. We left our field at Galatz. At 7 o'clock we ran into the clouds. At about 6,000 feet they were very heavy and thick, from 300 to 1,000 feet. We climbed through them and came out into the bright morning sunlight. It was a beautiful sight. This sea of clouds and the morning sunlight on them was an artist's dream for colour and softness. We headed towards Bukharest, travelling by compass only. We got the direction of the wind, to see if it was a cross wind and figure our drift— a strong cross wind will carry you quite a ways in a 100-mile trip. We had a wind about 1-4 N.W. so we didn't have much lift to worry about. It was impossible to see the earth. Our compass was all we could see.

We continued until we figured we were near Bukharest. Then we came down through the clouds to look around and get our bearings. As soon as we came out in the clear, below the clouds, we saw Bukharest about five miles ahead, and to the left of us. We had a look at Bukharest, then headed toward Nilkopo and Sofia. Always over the clouds at about 6,000 feet altitude. If it had not been for the clouds we would have been up 15,000 feet, but it was not necessary, as we could not be seen from below and there was no danger from guns.

We passed over one or two clear spots only a few hundred feet across. After we had gone along for about fifty minutes we came through the clouds again for the second town on our route. When we came out from under the clouds it was raining torrents and very difficult for us to see the earth at all. The rain was very disagreeable. It cut our faces at the rate of speed we travelled, so we did not see our town. We climbed back above the clouds again and continued toward Sofia under the same conditions, always cloudy.

At last we were due at Sofia, according to our watches, and the average speed we were making, about 120 miles per hour. We slowed our metres and came through the clouds to see if we could get our bearings from the earth and our maps. When we came out of the clouds we were just over the suburbs of Sofia. I think that was one of the best guesses I ever made. Not altogether a guess, of course. Our instruments are very accurate, but one's speed never is the same. You must judge for yourself, as there is no accurate speed metre for an aeroplane. We headed for the centre of the city, to locate the palace of King Ferdinand and the Parliament building. We had a plan of the city, so it did not take us long to find them.

Sofia is very interesting from the air; the way it is laid out is very peculiar. It is in the shape of a triangle, all streets terminating in an immense circle in the centre, where all the Government buildings are located. I chose the palace of the King; my comrade the House of Parliament. We got directly over them and came down in spirals.

STREET-FIGHTING IN PETROGRAD DURING THE REVOLUTION

I dropped my first bomb from about 3,000 feet. It struck the corner of the palace. I saw it explode, the smoke and dust flying up. I could see people running in all directions. My second one was a miss. It exploded in the court-yard about fifty feet from the palace. The third and last was a good hit on the top of the building. Whether or not it went through, I will not know until after the war. I hope it did! My comrade made good hits also. We saw the people picking up wounded and dead. We turned around, in about five minutes, and gave them an exhibition. If I had only had a machine gun I would have rid the world of some more scum. But we did not carry our guns, so as to be able to carry three bombs, otherwise we would only have been able to carry two.

They fired at us from below with rifles and machine guns, but we should worry about that!

After we got our results well summed up, we climbed and started back toward Nilkopo, Bukharest, and home.

As we got near the Roumanian frontier the weather began to clear and we could see the earth through the holes in the clouds. Before passing Bukharest it was clear. We climbed to about 4,000 feet and continued on our way. It was not long before we could see the Danube in the distance and as it loomed near we felt much relief, as to be captured in the Balkans means death. Our motors purred along and carried us safely back to our starting point. We only saw one enemy airplane that had been sent out to meet us. He was too low and did not cause us any trouble. We were unarmed so could not put up a fight. In case we were attacked our only defence would have been our skill and wits. They often answer the purpose.

We came down and landed at Galatz, on our field.

My comrade and I were congratulated by our superior officers and also by King Ferdinand of Roumania. We were very tired and hungry—the strain on a man is something beyond imagination. After a great lunch and a *siesta* we felt much better.

The route we had taken was as follows: Galatz following the railroad line to Braila, Bukharest, Nilkopo, and on to Sofia. The distance was 540 miles for the round trip. We made it in four hours and twenty minutes. After returning to Galatz we learned a few of the details but not much. In the bombing of the Parliament building one deputy had been killed and several notables wounded. The king's palace was badly damaged and some excitement was caused. We do not want to kill women and children as the Germans are doing in France and England. We want to clear them up fair and square and we will!

Now that the raid was over we had two days' leave. So we went to Jassy to see some pretty girls. We had a nice holiday and came back thoroughly contented and happy, and ready for another exploit.

CHAPTER 14

The Revolution as I Saw it

When I got back into Russia again and was travelling toward Petrograd, during the first days of March, I heard some talk of a revolution. The early rumours were mostly to the effect that the Church would not give the consent, but I was told that on the 10th the dignitaries sent out word to the people that God no longer loved the *Czar*. There were all kinds of proclamations, and on the 12th Nicholas signed his abdication of the throne. Then came the real revolution and with it more proclamations. There were proclamations plastered around everywhere until you couldn't see the walls, they were so thick.

One of them was directed to the army and told the men that they were free, that they were not required to salute their officers because they were only men like themselves. The discipline in the Russian army had been very severe, and you can imagine what followed. The majority of the officers belonged to the aristocracy and of course they resented this. Most of them were murdered and the rest disarmed; a great many escaped. The soldiers then proceeded to elect their own officers. Anyone who was a popular man in his company was elected as an officer.

Nearly all the Russian soldiers with whom I talked wanted the Grand Duke Nicholas for *Czar*. When they were told that there were no more grand dukes the soldiers said:

"Why, we didn't want him taken away. He was our friend."

As nearly as I could make out, about fifty *per cent*, of the soldiers went back to their homes. They believed that the revolution made them free to do anything they liked. There was virtually a verbal armistice by the troops that remained. The Germans gave the Russians plenty to drink. Often they would dance together and have a great time, saying that there was going to be no more war.

"We are all rich now; we don't have to work anymore," was the Russian belief.

The poor officers fared pretty badly, I can tell you. I saw them killed in cold blood by their troops. One, a general in Bessarahin, was hanged. He had gone into a railroad station to get something to eat. Some soldiers were making remarks which he resented. He then sent for an armed guard to arrest the men, but when the guard came they arrested the general instead. They took him out of the station and a crowd gathered round. Somebody said:

"What will we do with him?"

Then someone suggested, "Hang him." And they did.

This was absolutely uncalled-for, as he was a good man, was one of the few artillery experts in Russia.

In Petrograd things were just as bad. A friend of mine, a lady living at the Hotel du Nord, had an experience which is typical of the condition of the city at that time. The Hotel du Nord is just in front of the Nicholas station. She was awakened one morning by firing in the street and the station. She looked out to see what was the trouble, just in time to get the end of her nose shot off by a passing bullet. That is a good example of Russian marksmanship. When they are shooting at you, you are safe. But if they are shooting at something else, you had better hide.

You can guess what went on in a city of 3,000,000 population during a time like that, with no law and order. All the convicts were liberated, but some of them went back to the prison for protection. The people were taking everything they could get their hands on; most all the stores were closed. It was very difficult to get anything to eat and *rubles* were like pennies. Everyone was arrested about twice daily. But, with a few *rubles*, you were safe.

It was even more tragic and amusing to see the way in which

FUNERAL PROCESSION GOING TO THE CHAMP MARS, PETROGRAD

the Navy carried on its revolution. They were worse than the Army. The Baltic fleet was frozen in, so the sailors chopped holes in the ice and pushed their officers underneath. They said that by doing this they did not murder their officers, they only pushed them under. If they couldn't get out, it was not their fault, so they had clear consciences. The men also elected their officers. One day two greasy sailors walked into the bureau of the Navy at Petrograd and said:

"We are the commanders of the Baltic fleet."

The secretary thought that this was a bad proposition, but he said:

"Well, you men are very important, so we'll have to keep you here to be delegates in the Workingmen's and Soldiers' Senate."

I heard afterwards that some old reserve officers had to take command, men who had not been on a ship in twenty years.

Among the many changes in the Russian army brought about by the revolution is the giving of commissions to Jews. Before it there were no Jewish officers allowed in the army. Now they may have fifty *per cent*. This does not please the Russians.

I talked with many soldiers and every one of them had just one idea—he wanted to live in the Royal Palace. They told me that it was their right.

"The palaces belong to us now; why can't we live in them?"

You could buy almost any sort of army equipment you wanted on the streets of Petrograd. The soldiers were joyously selling everything that had been issued to them. If you wanted a motorcycle you could get it from a former army motorcyclist for 200 *rubles*. Why, you could even buy a cannon if you wanted it. The soldiers said:

"It all belongs to us now, after the revolution. We don't want to fight any more. Now we are going to enjoy our wealth so we don't want to fight any more and risk being killed."

These were almost unbelievable days in Petrograd. It was like boom times in a Western mining town in the United States, There was absolutely no standard of prices, everybody seemed bent on charging just a little more than anybody else. I paid $10 for a dinner in Petrograd just before I left, that would cost sixty cents in New York. However, no one seemed to mind it; everyone was rich. I never saw the equal, it seemed more like a gold strike than a war.

When I came to try to get away from Petrograd my real troubles began. The railroads were disorganized completely, absolutely no system. It took seven days to go seven hundred miles on a passenger train, and three months to get a goods train from Vladivostok to Petrograd. At first I decided to return by the same route I had come, going to Sweden, Christiania, Bergen and on to London. So, on the first day of May, I left Petrograd. I was able to get as far as Christiania, where I waited in vain for a boat. No one gave me any hope of getting to London, so I retraced my steps and returned to Petrograd. I was forced to make my homeward journey in the other direction, through Siberia, Manchuria, and Japan to San Francisco.

Never again for me in Russia!

BURYING THE DEAD AFTER THE REVOLUTION, THE CHAMP MARS, PETROGRAD

CHAPTER 15

My Pals

Many of the things which I am going to tell about my pals in the Foreign Legion and the Lafayette Escadrille happened after we broke up and got scattered, but no matter. This book would not be complete without some account of them. We were together more or less until the Boche got one after another of the bunch. A few of us are still here to get back at him. We were proud of being Americans, and that is why I want to tell the records of these men, the things which I saw and know about them. Much of it is not known on this side.

Charles Sweeney, one of my most loyal friends, was a brave and excellent soldier; he was very severely wounded during the offensive in Champagne in 1915. He won the rank of Captain, has been decorated with the *Legion d'Honneur* and the *Croix de Guerre*, twice mentioned in the orders of the entire army. He was recently transferred into the U. S. Army with the rank of Major. I think he should have been made a Brigadier-General as he is far in advance of many American officers in the science of modern warfare.

I don't think you could find a bigger-hearted man than Rene Philezot. He told me that he would leave his bones on the field of battle, and he did. Christmas day, 1914, René sent $400 from the trenches to the Belgians when many a millionaire living in a palace only gave a five-spot, and few did that. It's the difference in men, and the best are never known until it's too late.

Jimmy Bach was the son of a millionaire, but that didn't seem to hurt him any. Jimmy was one of the best. Absolutely fearless, a friend indeed. Jimmy was taken prisoner in the aviation in September, 1915, while performing a special mission, that of landing spies in the German lines. He had gone back to get a comrade who had met with an accident. Jimmy broke his propeller by striking a stump, was made prisoner and tried three times by a court-martial. He had one of the best attorneys in Berlin to defend him and was acquitted of being an accomplice of a spy, otherwise he would have been shot. I missed him very much, and I got revenge for him later on I am glad to say.

Stewart Carstairs, a slender, refined boy, was one of the gamest I ever knew. He was a very well-known artist. How he was able to resist hardship so wonderfully I never understood, for he suffered exceedingly from neuralgia. I have seen his face swollen twice its normal size, but never a complaint. He was one of our mysterious kind who always had cigarettes. I don't know how he got them, but I assure you that anyone with cigarettes was popular, especially with me. Stewart was forced to leave in February, 1915, on account of his health, but I admired him for holding out as long as he did.

Bill Thaw has been wounded in the elbow, but he is there yet flying every day with his left arm that cannot be straightened out. Only a few do those things, most of them would go home, and pose as a hero. Bill is my best friend, for I know what is in him. He ranks now as a lieutenant, has the *Legion d'Honneur, Croix de Guerre*, five citations in the Army orders and the last I heard he had brought down his eighth Boche. I don't think many people know how Bill Thaw got his wound. It happened this way. One day Thaw, Rockwell and myself were together over near Fort de Vaux when I attacked a German.

As I did so, two other Germans came after me. Thaw came to my aid, and he was hit by a German some three hundred yards away and below him. The shot took him in the left elbow. He went down and I got out of my difficulty and watched him. He landed in the second-line trenches, but did not break his machine. In landing the machine tore down all the telephone lines

GROUP TAKEN DAY OF NORMAN PRINCE'S FUNERAL.

Left to right: sitting—Berr Hall, Lieutenant de Laage, Captain Thenault, William Thaw, Father Armonier (father for the aviators), Sergeant Johnson. Standing—Rumsey, Pavelka, Marshall, Masson, Hill, Robert Rockwell. Whisky, our pet lion, is seen on Thaw's knees.

to the trenches in that sector.

He did not know whether he was in our lines or in the German lines. But as the soldiers came up he felt much better when he saw they were French. Balsy also, in his experience, did not know where he was. When hit in the stomach by an explosive bullet he said it was a terrible sensation and, as he came to, he righted his machine and kept saying to himself:

"Keep your head, boy, keep your head."

It was only by superhuman effort he landed. It was some bad ground and he wrecked his machine. He was soon picked up and taken to a field hospital where he was in a state of coma for four days, but owing to his good state of health he was saved.

James W. Ganson, who was a game sport, was forty-six years old when he enlisted. He hung on for a year, when, owing to ill health he had to give up. He tried to get transferred into the artillery, but was unsuccessful, so he went home.

Wilson was quite a diplomat. He didn't believe in work, and said he was a doctor, so Dr. Wilson he was. He was our chief chemist.

David King, a man of a well-known family and a fine chap, spent about two years in the trenches. He was wounded and badly gassed and has almost lost his sight. He was transferred to the artillery and is there yet.

J. J. Casey, an artist of note, and game, has been continually in the midst of it all. Casey has been wounded twice and is there now, looking for more.

E. Towle, of Tuxedo, was a game boy—only eighteen. He spent some months in the trenches, later got his release and came home.

Chatkoff, a wild and woolly chap, spent a number of months in the trenches, was transferred into the aviation and had some sport learning to fly. He had numerous accidents and finally asked to be sent to the trenches to rest his nerves. He came back a little later to fly and landed on a house-top, which ended his career as an aviator. Chatkoff has gone back to the trenches, saying that he is a better bayonet pilot.

Paul Rockwell, good old southern boy, came over to get revenge on the Germans, was badly wounded in May, 1915, and was released. Paul is now married to a beautiful French girl, Miss Legg, and I hope Paul is as good a husband as he was soldier.

One of the best of them all was poor Kiffin Rockwell, brother of Paul, one of the cleanest, squarest men I ever knew. Kiffin didn't know the meaning of fear. I think he had as many combats in the air as any man in the French aviation. He was credited with three Boches, but I am sure he brought down more, no less than six. He and I were not very popular with our captain, as we told him and everyone else what we thought. Kiffin lost his life in a combat near the spot where he brought down his first German. He wore the *Médaille Militaire*, the *Croix de Guerre*, and had the rank of Sub-Lieutenant. I still miss him and always will, and I have not yet finished revenging Kiffin's loss. He was so skinny, I used to call him the Living Hall Tree. We used to tell Kiffin that if he could keep side on to a German it would be impossible to hit him. He was a good poker player, a game at which we spent many pleasant evenings.

F. W. Zinn seemed like the laziest boy in the world, not lazy exactly but always tired, and one of the worst bookworms I ever saw. No matter where he was he always had a book of some sort. He tried flying but did not make a success. Later he developed into one of the best men in the photographic service in France.

Bob Soubirain, who spent eighteen months in the trenches, is now one of the good flyers in the aviation corps. He deserves the best of luck.

George Casmeze had the bad luck to be taken ill. He was the originator of the American Volunteer Corps, but had to be left behind.

Edgar J. Bouligny was the best specimen of a man I have ever seen. He was wounded several times but is still in the game. He was too heavy for the aviation, but he would have made a dandy fighter.

Bob Scanlon, was a negro prize fighter. He said he liked to

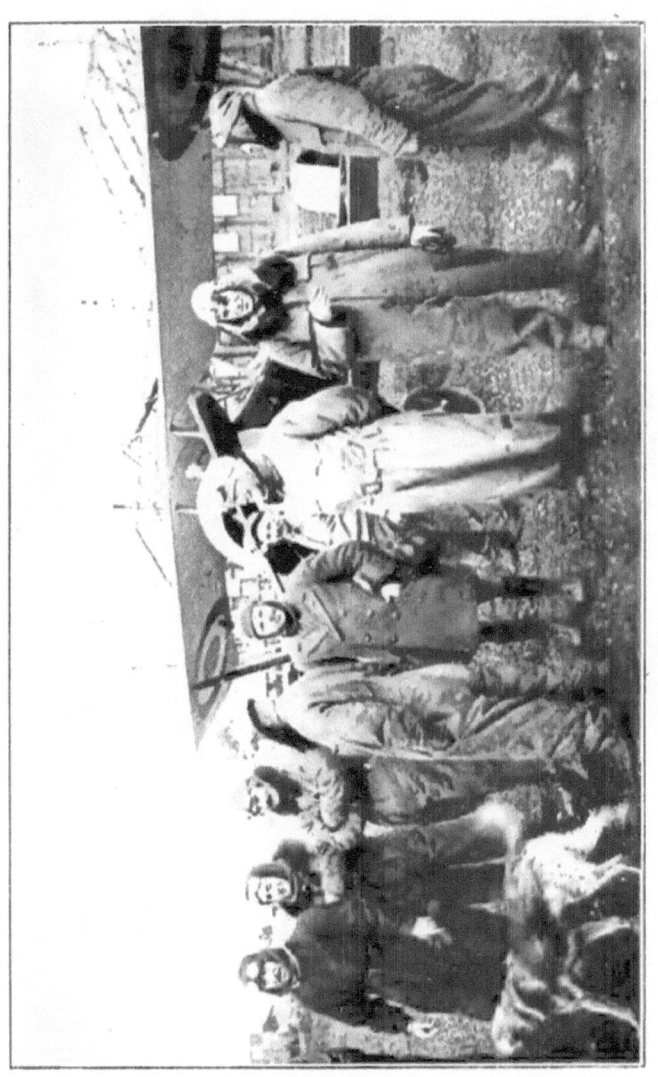

SAME GROUP IN FLYING-CLOTHES

Left to right: Cowdin, Hall, Thaw, De Laage, Prince, McConnell, Rockwell, Captain Thenault.

fight but preferred to pick his own ground. I don't know what became of him.

Dennis Dowd, a New York lawyer, spent eighteen months in the trenches, and then transferred to the Flying Corps. Dowd was killed last fall in an accident in his School.

George Del Peuch was a good fighter and very brave. I think he was killed at the Battle of the Somme, and I wager he died game. He was that kind.

F. Morlae, who was a reckless fellow but a fine soldier, went through the Battles of the Somme and Champagne. He came home to Los Angeles and died there from the shock of what he had been through.

F. Capdevielle is still in France, wounded twice. He wears the *Croix de Guerre*, Charles Trinkard is also at the front yet.

F. Landreaux spent a year or more there, and has since been released. He was one of our best entertainers, and was well known as an artist in France. He was always in poor health, but game, and I admired him very much.

Allen Segar, whose war poems are the best ever written, was a brave and fearless boy. His talent was unknown and undeveloped then. I understand a monument is to be erected to his memory in Paris. He was killed at the Battle of the Somme, as were some of the boys who came on later.

Norman Prince was one of the kind who wants to see others do well and get along. He looked after everyone but himself. He was the founder of the American Escadrille, and spent all his time making it go and finally did so. I liked Norman very much. He was a big loss to all of us as he was the one that furnished the pep for the outfit.

James McConnell was not only a fine boy, but a talented writer. I used to call him McScandal. I was sorry to hear of his death, for I think he would have written some very interesting stories on the war. I remember our first trip over the lines. He was lost and followed me all the time. He said I didn't know whether we were going to Berlin or Paris.

Charles Beaumont changed regiments and I don't know what

has become of him. E. H. Towle was taken ill and had to be left behind, poor fellow. He afterwards came back home.

Victor Chapman, the man of all men, was one of our bravest, and one of the best friends I ever had. A lover of art and of life, he was good in every way. He did three men's work daily and very rarely came in without a few bullet holes in his machine. He brought down at the least six Germans. He attacked them, no matter how many there were or what the conditions. He gave his life for humanity. At the time of his death he was carrying a deep scalp wound caused by a bullet ploughing its way through his scalp just above the right ear. An ordinary man would have been in the hospital, but not Victor. He was fond of art and reading, and with the latter he spent much of his spare time. He was very much interested in science, also, and did a good deal of shooting and walking. He was an exceptional conversationalist; he could interest you on almost any subject. Not like most of the boys, he was very settled in his habits, was never excited or mad, and I am confident he never knew what fear meant. He had spent a year in the trenches previous to entering the flying corps.

Wouldn't any American be proud to have lived and fought with a bunch like this!

LEONAUR

ALSO FROM LEONAUR

AVAILABLE IN SOFTCOVER OR HARDCOVER WITH DUST JACKET

WINGED WARFARE *by William A. Bishop*—The Experiences of a Canadian 'Ace' of the R.F.C. During the First World War.

THE STORY OF THE LAFAYETTE ESCADRILLE *by George Thenault*—A famous fighter squadron in the First World War by its commander..

R.F.C.H.Q. *by Maurice Baring*—The command & organisation of the British Air Force during the First World War in Europe.

SIXTY SQUADRON R.A.F. *by A. J. L. Scott*—On the Western Front During the First World War.

THE STRUGGLE IN THE AIR *by Charles C. Turner*—The Air War Over Europe During the First World War.

WITH THE FLYING SQUADRON *by H. Rosher*—Letters of a Pilot of the Royal Naval Air Service During the First World War.

OVER THE WEST FRONT *by "Spin" & "Contact"* —Two Accounts of British Pilots During the First World War in Europe, Short Flights With the Cloud Cavalry by "Spin" and Cavalry of the Clouds by "Contact".

SKYFIGHTERS OF FRANCE *by Henry Farré*—An account of the French War in the Air during the First World War.

THE HIGH ACES *by Laurence la Tourette Driggs*—French, American, British, Italian & Belgian pilots of the First World War 1914-18.

PLANE TALES OF THE SKIES *by Wilfred Theodore Blake*—The experiences of pilots over the Western Front during the Great War.

IN THE CLOUDS ABOVE BAGHDAD *by J. E. Tennant*—Recollections of the R. F. C. in Mesopotamia during the First World War against the Turks.

THE SPIDER WEB *by P. I. X. (Theodore Douglas Hallam)*—Royal Navy Air Service Flying Boat Operations During the First World War by a Flight Commander

EAGLES OVER THE TRENCHES *by James R. McConnell & William B. Perry*—Two First Hand Accounts of the American Escadrille at War in the Air During World War 1-Flying For France: With the American Escadrille at Verdun and Our Pilots in the Air

KNIGHTS OF THE AIR *by Bennett A. Molter*—An American Pilot's View of the Aerial War of the French Squadrons During the First World War.

LEONAUR

ALSO FROM LEONAUR

A HISTORY OF THE 17TH AERO SQUADRON *by Frederick Mortimer Clapp*—An American Squadron on the Western Front During the First World War.

RICHTHOFEN & BOELCKE IN THEIR OWN WORDS *by Manfred Freiher von Richthofen & Oswald Böelcke*—The Red Battle Flyer by Manfred Freiher von Richthofen and An Aviator's Field Book by Oswald Böelcke.

WITH THE FRENCH FLYING CORPS *by Carroll Dana Winslow*—The Experiences of an American Pilot During the First World War.

"AMBULANCE 464" ENCORE DES BLESSÉS *by Julien H. Bryan*—The experiences of an American Volunteer with the French Army during the First World War

THE GREAT WAR IN THE MIDDLE EAST: 1 *by W. T. Massey*—The Desert Campaigns & How Jerusalem Was Won---two classic accounts in one volume.

THE GREAT WAR IN THE MIDDLE EAST: 2 *by W. T. Massey*—Allenby's Final Triumph.

SMITH-DORRIEN *by Horace Smith-Dorrien*—Isandlwhana to the Great War.

1914 *by Sir John French*—The Early Campaigns of the Great War by the British Commander.

GRENADIER *by E. R. M. Fryer*—The Recollections of an Officer of the Grenadier Guards throughout the Great War on the Western Front.

BATTLE, CAPTURE & ESCAPE *by George Pearson*—The Experiences of a Canadian Light Infantryman During the Great War.

DIGGERS AT WAR *by R. Hugh Knyvett & G. P. Cuttriss*—"Over There" With the Australians by R. Hugh Knyvett and Over the Top With the Third Australian Division by G. P. Cuttriss. Accounts of Australians During the Great War in the Middle East, at Gallipoli and on the Western Front.

HEAVY FIGHTING BEFORE US *by George Brenton Laurie*—The Letters of an Officer of the Royal Irish Rifles on the Western Front During the Great War.

THE CAMELIERS *by Oliver Hogue*—A Classic Account of the Australians of the Imperial Camel Corps During the First World War in the Middle East.

RED DUST *by Donald Black*—A Classic Account of Australian Light Horsemen in Palestine During the First World War.

LEONAUR

ALSO FROM LEONAUR
AVAILABLE IN SOFTCOVER OR HARDCOVER WITH DUST JACKET

FARAWAY CAMPAIGN *by F. James*—Experiences of an Indian Army Cavalry Officer in Persia & Russia During the Great War.

REVOLT IN THE DESERT *by T. E. Lawrence*—An account of the experiences of one remarkable British officer's war from his own perspective.

MACHINE-GUN SQUADRON *by A. M. G.*—The 20th Machine Gunners from British Yeomanry Regiments in the Middle East Campaign of the First World War.

A GUNNER'S CRUSADE *by Antony Bluett*—The Campaign in the Desert, Palestine & Syria as Experienced by the Honourable Artillery Company During the Great War .

DESPATCH RIDER *by W. H. L. Watson*—The Experiences of a British Army Motorcycle Despatch Rider During the Opening Battles of the Great War in Europe.

TIGERS ALONG THE TIGRIS *by E. J. Thompson*—The Leicestershire Regiment in Mesopotamia During the First World War.

HEARTS & DRAGONS *by Charles R. M. F. Crutwell*—The 4th Royal Berkshire Regiment in France and Italy During the Great War, 1914-1918.

INFANTRY BRIGADE: 1914 *by John Ward*—The Diary of a Commander of the 15th Infantry Brigade, 5th Division, British Army, During the Retreat from Mons.

DOING OUR 'BIT' *by Ian Hay*—Two Classic Accounts of the Men of Kitchener's 'New Army' During the Great War including *The First 100,000 & All In It*.

AN EYE IN THE STORM *by Arthur Ruhl*—An American War Correspondent's Experiences of the First World War from the Western Front to Gallipoli-and Beyond.

STAND & FALL *by Joe Cassells*—With the Middlesex Regiment Against the Bolsheviks 1918-19.

RIFLEMAN MACGILL'S WAR *by Patrick MacGill*—A Soldier of the London Irish During the Great War in Europe including *The Amateur Army*, *The Red Horizon* & *The Great Push*.

WITH THE GUNS *by C. A. Rose & Hugh Dalton*—Two First Hand Accounts of British Gunners at War in Europe During World War 1- Three Years in France with the Guns and With the British Guns in Italy.

THE BUSH WAR DOCTOR *by Robert V. Dolbey*—The Experiences of a British Army Doctor During the East African Campaign of the First World War.

LEONAUR

ALSO FROM LEONAUR
AVAILABLE IN SOFTCOVER OR HARDCOVER WITH DUST JACKET

THE 9TH—THE KING'S (LIVERPOOL REGIMENT) IN THE GREAT WAR 1914 - 1918 *by Enos H. G. Roberts*—Mersey to mud—war and Liverpool men.

THE GAMBARDIER *by Mark Severn*—The experiences of a battery of Heavy artillery on the Western Front during the First World War.

FROM MESSINES TO THIRD YPRES *by Thomas Floyd*—A personal account of the First World War on the Western front by a 2/5th Lancashire Fusilier.

THE IRISH GUARDS IN THE GREAT WAR - VOLUME 1 *by Rudyard Kipling*—Edited and Compiled from Their Diaries and Papers—The First Battalion.

THE IRISH GUARDS IN THE GREAT WAR - VOLUME 1 *by Rudyard Kipling*—Edited and Compiled from Their Diaries and Papers—The Second Battalion.

ARMOURED CARS IN EDEN *by K. Roosevelt*—An American President's son serving in Rolls Royce armoured cars with the British in Mesopatamia & with the American Artillery in France during the First World War.

CHASSEUR OF 1914 *by Marcel Dupont*—Experiences of the twilight of the French Light Cavalry by a young officer during the early battles of the great war in Europe.

TROOP HORSE & TRENCH *by R.A. Lloyd*—The experiences of a British Lifeguardsman of the household cavalry fighting on the western front during the First World War 1914-18.

THE EAST AFRICAN MOUNTED RIFLES *by C.J. Wilson*—Experiences of the campaign in the East African bush during the First World War.

THE LONG PATROL *by George Berrie*—A Novel of Light Horsemen from Gallipoli to the Palestine campaign of the First World War.

THE FIGHTING CAMELIERS *by Frank Reid*—The exploits of the Imperial Camel Corps in the desert and Palestine campaigns of the First World War.

STEEL CHARIOTS IN THE DESERT *by S. C. Rolls*—The first world war experiences of a Rolls Royce armoured car driver with the Duke of Westminster in Libya and in Arabia with T.E. Lawrence.

WITH THE IMPERIAL CAMEL CORPS IN THE GREAT WAR *by Geoffrey Inchbald*—The story of a serving officer with the British 2nd battalion against the Senussi and during the Palestine campaign.